A FRESH LOOK AT
PENTECOST
IN LIGHT OF
PRESENT-DAY CONFUSION

By
William J. Finnigan

A Fresh Look at Pentecost in Light of Present Day Confusion
© William J. Finnigan, D. Min.
September 2021

Printed in the United States of America
ISBN: 978-1-7371005-6-0

Formatting, Editing and Publishing Assistance By:
The Old Paths Publications, Inc.
Cleveland, Ga 30528
www.theoldpathspublications.com
email: TOP@theoldpathspublications.com

1.0

DEDICATION

To my Beloved brother in Christ, Robert (Bob) Quesenbury, I dedicate this book. You taught me from our college days how to love God's Word and walk with Him. In many times of trouble, you have wisely used your wealth of Scriptural knowledge and godly hymns to minister special "healing" to me. Thank you for being such a faithful, loving friend and fellow servant. I honor you

PREFACE

Jesus said,

> "...Upon this rock I will built my church; and the gates of Hell shall not prevail against it." (Matt. 16:18)

The Psalmist exclaims (prophetically):

> "Behold, how good and how pleasant it is for brethren to dwell together in unity... for there the Lord commanded the blessing, even life for evermore." (Psa. 133:1, 3)

The Apostle Paul exhorts:

> With all lowliness and meekness, with longsuffering, forbearing one another in love; Endeavouring to keep the unity of the Spirit in the bond of peace. There is one body, and one Spirit, even as ye are called in one hope of your calling; One Lord, one faith, one baptism, One God and Father of all, who is above all, and through all, and in you all. (Eph. 4:2-6)

Those who have been reconciled to God through Christ the Redeemer have also been joined to each other in unity. We are "one body," having "one Spirit" and "one baptism." That is a biblical fact, whether we'll have it or not. It is amazing to me the number of "separated brethren" there are who are "separated" for the wrong reasons. Separation from the world is one thing, but separation from true believers is another.

The same Devil that "unifies" the ungodly, divides the godly. Wesley and Whitefield, of Great Awakening fame (1730s), often "argued" over certain Scriptures, agreeing to

7

disagree; but that didn't dampen their love for God, for each other, for the brethren, and for lost souls. Some today are looking for a "denominational revival" in order to promote their own group or bias agenda; but Christ is "building His Church," His Body of true believers, regardless of their denominational "name tag."

The next "awakening" may come in the midst of political persecution, where true saints will be brought together in "revived" spiritual love (Gal. 5:22&23). People of different theological persuasions will find themselves fellowshipping together around the Lord Jesus Christ Himself and His infallible Word (the Bible). This scenario is presently a reality in some communist countries where souls are being saved in spite of the Bible being outlawed. Thankfully, the Word is not bound!

False teaching and confusion have progressively "eaten away" at the core of true Christian unity. For instance, the so-called "full gospel" or the Charismatic teaching of a "second baptism (blessing)" evidenced by "tongues-speaking" has greatly fractured Christ's Body; the enemy has cleverly used it to divide believers between the "haves" and the "have nots." Then there's a "hyper-charismatic" teaching called the "prosperity gospel" with its spurious emphasis on a sure "promise" of "health and wealth" to those who "have faith." I challenge these teachings in light of the Scriptures. In addition, the age-old teaching of "replacement theology," (i.e. Israel's being replaced by the Church) is also Biblically explored.

I submit that the majority of erroneous teachings that have invaded the Church are due to a faulty understanding of Pentecost. This pertains to charismatics and non-charismatics alike; whether we're addressing "wild-fire" or "no fire!" The dispensing of the Holy Spirit on that Day fulfilled and "reformed" forever God's program of the ages. The Acts of the Holy Spirit portray His coming to dwell in the bodies of believing Jews and Gentiles alike; and by His "baptism of the Spirit" (1 Cor. 12:13) one unified Body of Christ was established. Now we need a new-breed of Spirit-filled preachers who love God and the brethren, while they accurately and compassionately proclaim the whole counsel of God!.

I invite you to join me as we explore this glorious subject of Pentecost. I pray that some of the age-old misconceptions that have unduly divided true believers for centuries might be reevaluated Scripturally; and that the Spirit of Pentecost would be pleased to revive and biblically unify His Church; in turn, may this spark a profound spiritual awakening in our country prior to His Second Coming! Even so, come, Lord Jesus!

WJF

TABLE OF CONTENTS

INTRODUCTION

Personal Confession and Burden

If there's been any controversy that has profoundly divided the true Christian Church, it is the question and understanding of what really happened on the Day of Pentecost. This subject is basic to a correct understanding of how the Church began and the subsequent teachings and practices taking us to the present day. To say that there have been divisions, confusion, and even militant misunderstanding, is an understatement.

Theological controversies like God's Sovereignty vs. man's free will, and the theories regarding Eschatology (study of last-day events) continue to warrant great interest, and rightly so; but the proper understanding and application of Pentecost is also of vital importance in the lives of believers today. In my opinion, the controversy that surrounds this subject must be further explored Biblically, especially as it relates to the Body of Christ.

Let it be said that the thrust of this book is geared toward genuine, Bible-believing, regenerated Christians, who have already settled on the Cardinal Truths of Scripture. We are not discussing here the fundamental teachings of the Lord Jesus Christ, embraced by every true believer; e.g. Christ's virgin birth, His deity (the God-Man); His Blood atonement (death) for sinners on the Cross; His bodily resurrection from the tomb; His ascension to Heaven; His Second Coming in Glory, etc. These are teachings (doctrines) subscribed by all true believers in Christ. In fact, Paul speaks of "forbearing one another in love; endeavoring to *keep the unity of the Spirit* in the bond of peace; there is one body, and one Spirit...one Lord, one faith, *one baptism*; one God and Father of all..." (Eph.4:2-6; italics mine)

Notice that he exhorts us to "*keep* the unity of the Spirit which He (the Spirit) has already made. We cannot keep something we don't have. This truth of "one Body" has somehow been "lost in the shuffle" as evidenced by those who gloat in our differences rather than our unity. There *is* a valid, Biblical ecumenism based on the aforementioned Fundamentals of the Faith. I think we're apt to experience the reality of this unity anew if the forces of Hell around the world continue to mount against true Christianity.

Right now persecuted saints under the "boot" of Communism and/or Islam are not debating the "mode of baptism," for instance; but are seeking consolation with fellow believers who love Jesus and are "washed in the Blood of the Lamb!" They know that if they don't hang together, they'll hang separately. That doesn't mean that all believers are to sing in unison doctrinally, but rather sing in harmony as members of the Body of Christ. You remember how Jesus rebuked the disciples when they displayed their haughty, exclusivist attitude toward a fellow preacher who wasn't part of the "group." (cf. Lk. 9:46f) Certainly they were the elites ("the greatest") and how could that "independent" guy possibly be serving the Lord. But Jesus said: "Forbid him not; for he that is not against us is for us." God still has His humble, unrecognized servants planted around the world.

Understanding Pentecost

Our consideration centers on an event in Biblical history which has fostered debate, controversy and division for centuries among choice leaders of the Church. Pentecost was a Hebrew feast day recorded in Acts 2:1f, meaning 50 days past the celebration of Christ's Passion or Crucifixion.

What was this celebration about? What kind of people were there? What was the purpose and results? How is it to be interpreted and/or applied by God's people today? (e.g. rules of interpretation & context). What actually happened on that day? Must we go back to Pentecost again today? Could there be an even greater and progressive work in the believer's life now because of the provisions of Pentecost? These are valid questions that must be addressed in the context of this Biblical event.

It's been heart-rending to witness the ongoing, almost combative division in the Body of Christ over this issue. Extremes exist everywhere. Not to put all the blame on him, but Satan has done a masterful work of deception and confusion in the Church. (cf. Eph. 6:10f. etc.) Godly people have lined up on opposite sides, ready to fight to the death in propagating and/or defending their "biblical" position on the "gifts and power" of the Holy Spirit. Yet, the Spirit comes as a Comforter (Dove), not to divide God's children, but to unify us! The Holy Spirit didn't come to be "argued about," but to reveal Christ in a way otherwise impossible. My mentor, Dr. James A. Stewart, a missionary/evangelist of a generation past, used to say that "the Holy Ghost is too precious to be argued over."

CHAPTER 1
VISION OF TRUE UNITY

Could it be that God's saints who have bickered over the so-called "Pentecostal experience," may have done so out of ignorance and/or misinterpretation of Scripture? Has the "unity" of the Body of Christ (Eph. 4:1-7) been unduly hindered and rendered dysfunctional over truths that should have had the opposite effect? Or is it just a matter of whether one "believes in the gifts" or not? Is the whole thrust of "Pentecostal power" centered on "speaking in tongues" and/or "physical healing"? On the other hand, can I have the power of the Holy Spirit in my life, without embracing the so-called "baptism of the Spirit," as explained in Pentecostal and/or Charismatic circles? We need to take a hard look at these all-important and relative issues. The health and effectiveness of the Church of the Living God is at stake here; especially in light of the moral, political, and religious corruption that we face, while awaiting the "glorious appearing of the Great God and our Saviour, Jesus Christ!" (Titus 2:13)

No Axe to Grind

This is not a book about "taking sides" or proving a "point" at any cost. Nor is it an attempt to simply refute century-old denominational and theological traditions. I'm not even arguing for or against the so-called "Cessation" position (ceasing of certain gifts) or the "Continuance" (present validity of all gifts) position. While some proclaim the so-called "Full Gospel," others despise the term; yet could it be that there may be a "fuller Gospel" that goes beyond the event that happened at Pentecost? (Acts 2:1ff) Is it possible that we've been ignorant of a greater, progressive work of the Spirit since Pentecost?

Moreover, this will not be a footnoted, technical thesis to foster a bias, "finger-pointing" agenda; rather it is a fresh look at the

Scriptures, hopefully in context, attempting to address a critical and overdue problem in the true Church of Christ. This work is the result of a deep burden to clarify some colossal misinterpretations and confusion which, I believe, have been perpetrated and motivated by Satan. True believers have been unduly divided for too long!

What Does the Bible Say?

Having contemplated this subject of the true meaning of Pentecost for many decades, I humbly submit my findings. Like the proverbial sports referee, I must live with the reality that my "judgment calls" will please some, and upset others. The main issue is: "What does the Scripture teach?" What is God saying to us, and are we "rightly dividing (allocating) the Word of Truth?"

CHAPTER 2

THE PROBLEM OF MISINTERPRETATION OF THE SCRIPTURES

How much teaching today is based on a clear understanding of Biblical interpretation? "Interpretation" is defined as the power of explaining; to mediate understanding of a text between two parties. There are rules of interpretation that must be following in order to rightly represent and explain the author's meaning. While the entire Bible is written *for* us, it is not necessarily written *to* us. We may be guilty of "reading someone else's mail;" i.e. forcing the passage to apply directly to us, when it was specifically for someone else. The local post office may receive a truckload of mail, but it's not for everyone in the community. It has to be sorted out and then delivered to the designated parties; i.e. the name on the envelope needs to match the recipient.

To Whom is God Speaking?

For instance, when God gave Moses the land of Canaan it was a literal territory to establish an earthly nation (Israel) under His (God's) direct rule (theocracy). The New Testament Church has no such earthly possession, such as "a land flowing with milk and honey;" rather we are a heavenly people possessed with spiritual provision (cf. Eph. 1:3; Col. 3:1f). It's true that Christians own houses and lands on earth, but their "conversation [citizenship] is in Heaven." (cf. Phil. 3:20).

So-called "prosperity teachers" constantly focus on Deut. 28 to "prove" God's promise of ongoing (guarantied) "health and wealth" to the faithful Christian. It's true that the Lord promised abundant, tangible "blessings" upon Israel if they obeyed His law; but likewise, the "curses" of God's judgment upon the disobedient are also listed in the same passage. This cannot be ignored.

If the Mosaic Covenant is for today's saints, then we're in big trouble. We can't have it both ways; preaching the blessings, without warning of the impending curses is dishonest and erroneous. This was given specifically to Israel in an earthly covenant relationship with God. To "interpret" this as pertaining to the New Testament Church is "wrongly" dividing the Word of Truth. Are there legitimate applications for us today? Yes, by all means; but the Church is not Israel, and we are "reading their mail" (O.T.), which was sent directly to them. We are under the New Covenant, where all the types and shadows of Christ's redemption have been fulfilled. We are a body of called-out believers, blessed with "all spiritual blessings in the heavenlies." (Eph.1:3) Plus the fact, "There is therefore *now* no condemnation to them which are in Christ Jesus..." (Rom. 8:1) Hebrews makes it clear that the Mosaic system was "good", but Christ and His completed work is "better." (cf. Heb. 7:22-28) Amen!

Surely, the opening of the Red Sea (Ex. 14) is a beautiful picture of God's salvation and delivering power to us, but that event stands alone as a historic event; there's no way for us to return to that scene and expect God to literally part that Sea again. Rather, that glorious event displayed God's sovereign power and purpose in bringing deliverance to Israel in preparation for their establishment as a theocracy. We must reiterate that the Old Testament is a Jewish Book, featuring God's chosen, earthly people. Their laws, sacrifices, feast days, etc. all have meaning and application to the Church today, but were given exclusively to Israel, not to New Testament saints; however, there's definitely a progressive revelation here, from Moses to Jesus. The same God that gave Moses the Law (Exodus 20) to govern a nation was the same God who eventually gave Himself to fulfill that Law and to satisfy its (the Law's) Judgment upon sin.

By the same token, a New Testament believer would be hard pressed to cite the Passover celebration of Exodus 12 as the basis of his salvation. While that spotless lamb's blood was shed and applied to the Israelite's doorpost, it was unique to his redemption and forgiveness. This was repeated every year. They were saved "by faith", according to God's revelation, but the animal's blood could not "take away sin". (cf. John 1:29) Significantly, the Passover became a type of the future, completed work of the Passover Lamb on the Cross. The writer of Hebrews explains how Christ's sacrifice superseded the blood of "bulls and goats;" instead, "by His own blood He entered in **once** into the holy place, having obtained eternal redemption for us (Heb. 9:12; emphasis mine)." The Passover is completely fulfilled in Jesus Christ, and we cannot look back. We now have the Substance, rather than the "shadow!" They are not the same. To confuse these two elements is to misinterpret Scripture.

Israel is Not the Church

The same God who gave Moses the Law (Ex.20ff), was the same God who gave the Apostle Paul the Gospel of Grace (cf. 1Cor. 15:1-4). As mentioned above, the "law was given to Moses, but grace and truth came by Jesus Christ (John. 1:17). This does not mean that "grace and truth" contradicted the Law, but was rather a progression of God's revelation and fulfillment of the Old Testament legal system. That "progression," however, does not infer or conclude that the Church "replaces" Israel, who still has a future in God's economy (cf. Rom. 11:1-2). Spiritual Israel is blinded in this dispensation with the exception of a remnant of Jews who continue to believe in Jesus as the Messiah. When, as a nation, they rejected Jesus the Christ (Messiah), God opened the door of Salvation to the Gentiles (primarily through Paul; e.g. Acts 9ff). The unchanging, almighty God continues to move among men as He chooses, dispensing (ministering) His Sovereign and eternal plan.

Is it Faith or Presumption?

Moreover, the idea, held by some "faith" teachers, that we can take any promise of Scripture and indiscriminately "name it and claim it" is presumptuous, at best; e.g. Joshua's promised collapse of Jericho by walking around the city for seven days does not give the church credence today to "claim" a city for Christ by "prayer walking" or some such strategy. Neither the context nor God's purpose warrants such action. Jericho's literal, demise under God's judgment is a far cry from any literal attempt of "winning" a city for Christ! I can understand one's sincerity in such an attempt, but it's Biblically misguided.

Certainly there's a legitimate spiritual *application* here for exercising prayerful intercession for a city; but individuals still need to be confronted with the saving Gospel of Christ! (e.g. 1 Cor.15:2-4; Rom. 10:9&10)) This is not a "name it, claim it" situation; no more than those preachers who boldly "declared" the immediate termination of a recent Viral pandemic! Their failure was a display of foolish arrogance and deception; but such "false prophesies" and other erroneous "tactics" are prevalent in "Word of Faith" circles.

In these last days, we must get back to basics, as Paul reminds us in 2 Timothy 4:2-5:

> Preach the word; be instant in season, out of season; reprove, rebuke, exhort with all longsuffering and doctrine. For the time will come when they will not endure sound doctrine; but after their own lusts shall they heap to themselves teachers, having itching ears; And they shall turn away their ears from the truth, and shall be turned unto fables. But watch thou in all things, *endure afflictions, do the work of an*

evangelist, make full proof of thy ministry.
(emphasis mine)

Yes, it still pleases God "by the foolishness of preaching to save them that believe" (1 Cor.1:21).

In the same vein, we're told that Pentecost insures that every believer can "claim" spiritual and physical "prosperity." The inference is that a "poor" and/or "sick" Christian is lacking faith. This "prosperity gospel" teaches that a Spirit-filled believer has "authority by faith" to "name and claim" every blessing in the Book! That is like "ordering" God by just "ringing the bell" and expecting Him to come running like some "heavenly bell-hop." What kind of arrogance is this? The truth is that it is **God** who "rings the bell" and *we* "come running!" Certainly the Lord wants His children to prosper, but it may have little to do with the material realm; it (prosperity) is always connected to the Word and our obedience. (cf.Ps.1:3; Josh. 1:8; Matt. 6:33)

Faith takes God at His Word, like those in the Roll-call of Faith (cf. Heb. 11), with no thought of manipulating His "promises" for selfish or prideful gain. In fact, this same passage speaks not only of those who "through faith subdued kingdoms... (and) stopped the mouths of lions," but other saints that were "stoned...sawn asunder, being destitute, afflicted and tormented." (cf. Heb. 11:33-38) If this "health and wealth" gospel is true, it will work in places like Ethiopia, but it doesn't. The true Gospel of God's redeeming Grace will work *anywhere* in the world! Amen.

Understanding God's Timing and Purpose

There's a sense in which we can't even go back to the Cross. That was a once-and-for all event in History. When Jesus cried: "It is finished," all that was necessary to pay for sin's redemption was completed, never to be repeated again. (Heb. 10) When a sinner "goes to the Cross" to be saved from sin,

Christ doesn't reenact the Cross-work per se; instead, the Holy Spirit *applies* that finished, saving work to the sinner's believing heart.

Let's be clear, God is able to perform or repeat any miracle He chooses. As mentioned above, some "stopped the mouths of lions," like Daniel of old; yet, many saints since have been thrown to the lions with no seeming divine intervention. Why? In context, God decided to "deliver" Daniel from the lion's den to fulfill His purposes in Babylon. For whatever reason, that hasn't been the case for other believers. That doesn't mean that Daniel had more "faith" than those who didn't escape from the "lion's jaw."

Likewise in Acts 12, King Herod killed the Apostle James with the sword, trying to gain the favor of the Jews (vs. 2&3); yet Herod's attempt to destroy Peter failed when God delivered him from the inner prison, "secured" by two soldiers (vs.6). Yes, the Angel of the Lord led Peter out to freedom, while a group of believers were praying at Mary's house (vs. 12f). Why did God spare Peter and not James? Certainly it had nothing to do with James' lack of faith or the Lord's inability to rescue him; rather it had everything to do with God's ongoing purpose for Peter, who prepared the way, among other things, for Paul's ministry of the Gospel of Grace (e.g. Cornelius' conversion in Acts. 10).

I recently heard an analogy which helps to sum up the problem; we have arbitrarily taken Scriptures out of their context and mixed them together in a "theological blender," hoping for doctrinal clarity. Instead, the "ingredients" have proved to be incompatible, not "mixing" properly. The resultant product has been anything but spiritually "smooth" and palatable. Needless to say, this process has resulted in utter confusion and false interpretation.

CHAPTER 3
PRINCIPLES OF INTERPRETATION ESSENTIAL

Proper interpretation (understanding) of the Bible in its context is critical. Just like any other book, the author has a subject and audience in mind. How much more did God reveal His plan and purpose for particular people in a particular circumstance? For instance, the O.T. prophesies of Messiah were given primarily to Israel, not to the Gentiles (non-Jews); however, when they (Jews) rejected Him the door of grace was opened to Gentiles. John says, "He came unto *his own* [Israel], and his own received him not. But to as many as received him, to them gave he power to become the sons of God..." (John 1:11-12; emphasis mine)

All Scripture Written *for* Us, but Not *to* Us

Preachers galore are confusing *interpretation* with *application*. There is basically only one interpretation of any passage of Scripture in its context, but there can be many proper applications. Every passage of Scripture has a setting, purpose, etc.; there are specific people and unique circumstances involved, preventing that Scripture from being directly applied universally and at all times. For instance, the Bible is basically a Jewish book, written exclusively to and by Jews. (Luke was a Greek, but probably became a Hellenic Jew) The Old Testament primarily focuses on God's dealings with Israel, with some exceptions (e.g. Jonah and Nineveh). After the Gospels, the main thrust of the New Testament is the Gospel of Grace toward the gentiles, with corresponding exceptions of Jewish converts to Christ. So we must conclude that while the Bible is definitely written **for** us, it is not all written **to** us.

Ignoring this hermeneutic principle has been the source of much confusion and erroneous teaching in the Church. It was Miles

Coverdale, the English puritan scholar, who printed the first complete English translation of the Bible in 1535. He was a mighty preacher and renown student who left us with the following bed-rock principle for interpreting the Bible:

> *It shall greatly help you to understand Scripture if you mark not only what is spoken or written, but ask of whom and to whom, with what words, at what time, where, to what intent, with what circumstances, considering what goes before and what comes after.* (emphasis mine)

Rightly Dividing the Word of Truth

Foundational Examples:
Paul's admonition: 2 Timothy 2:15: "Study to shew thyself approved unto God, a workman that needeth not to be ashamed, rightly dividing the word of truth

2 Timothy 3:16, 17:

> All scripture is given by inspiration of God, and is profitable for doctrine, for reproof, for correction, for instruction in righteousness: That the man of God may be perfect, throughly furnished unto all good works.

Peter's instruction: 2 Peter 1:20, 21:

> Knowing this first, that no prophecy of the scripture is of any private interpretation. For the prophecy came not in old time by the will of man; but holy men of God spake as they were moved by the Holy Ghost.

2Pet 3:15, 16:

> And account that the longsuffering of our Lord is salvation; even as *our beloved brother Paul* also according to the wisdom given unto him *hath written unto you. As also in all his epistles, speaking in them of these things; in which are some things hard to be understood*, which they that are unlearned and unstable wrest, as they do also the other scriptures,, unto their own destruction. (emphasis mine)

Significantly, Peter here corroborates with and commends Paul's epistles to his flock, admitting that some things were "hard to be understood." He (Peter) readily acknowledges that Paul's letters would wisely confront and rectify those (Judaizers?) who were "wresting' or perverting Scripture. The word "wrest," according to Vincent, is used only here to depict a torture rack, where the limbs are twisted and dislocated. This could refer to Paul's solemn warning to those not preaching the Gospel of Grace (cf. Gal. 1:6-9). Remember that Peter and Paul were now on "the same page" regarding salvation in Christ alone by faith alone (plus nothing). Cf. Acts 15:5-11); however, I submit that Peter did not fully understand the "mystery of the church" as did Paul.

In this day of compromise and relevancy, we must never forget that God *has* spoken through His Eternal Word. We must never judge His Word by what we think or feel; but rather we must judge what we think and feel by His Word! How lightly we treat the Word these days, almost as though we're dealing with an ordinary book written by mere men. Certainly God used the instrumentality of human authors to pen His Word, but these were "holy men" on a unique mission, being "moved by the Holy Ghost." They wrote infallibly through the Infallible Spirit to give us the Infallible Scriptures! In some inexplicable way, under the Holy Spirit's control, the written words of these chosen men became the words of God. Through their instrumentality God gave all that He wanted us to know; namely the Bible, His **Manual** given to His creation.

Someone has written a brief but powerful challenge to humanity regarding the uniqueness of the Bible; it's entitled "The Word of God."

> This book contains the mind of God, the state of man, the way of Salvation, the doom of sinners, and the happiness of believers. Its doctrines are holy, its precepts are binding, its histories are true, and its decisions are immutable.
>
> Read it to be wise, believe it to be safe, and practice it to be holy. It contains light to direct you, food to support you, and comfort to cheer you. It is the traveler's map, the pilgrim's staff, the pilot's compass, the soldier's sword, and the Christian's charter.
>
> Here paradise is restored, Heaven opened, and the gates of Hell disclosed. Christ is its grand Object; our good is its design, and the glory of God its end.
>
> It should fill the memory, rule the heart, and guide the feet. Read it slowly frequently, and prayerfully. It is given to you in life, and will be opened in the judgment, and will be remembered forever. It involves the highest responsibility, will reward the greatest labor, and will condemn all who trifle with its sacred contents.
>
> -----Unknown

Believer's Connection with Inspiration

Remember, "**All** Scripture is given by inspiration of God…" (lit. "God-breathed") Just as He "breathed …the breath of life" into the first man, Adam (Gen. 2:7), so God "breathed spiritual life" into the Scriptures. That's why, unlike any other book, the Bible is **alive**, and able to impart eternal life to those who believe! Peter describes believers as "Being born again, not of corruptible seed, but of incorruptible, by the word of God, which *liveth* and abideth forever" (1 Pet. 1:23). (cf. John 5:24; 6:63)

The Scripture deals with every aspect of our lives. It was written exactly the way God intended, word for word, with no mistakes. It is "profitable for doctrine [godly teaching], for reproof, for correction, for instruction in righteousness (right living)"; furthermore, it equips the believer to fulfill the purpose for which God called him. (cf. 2 Tim. 3:16&17; Eph. 2: 8-10)) Someone commented that when you get close to the Bible you're "bumping up against God." Amen!

Some folks fail to read the Bible claiming they "can't understand it." Remember, this is God's eternal Word whose spiritual truth is unknowable apart from knowing the God who gave it. Paul says, "the natural [unsaved] man receiveth not the things of the Spirit of God...neither can he know them, because they are spiritually discerned." (1 Cor. 2:14) That's why mere intelligence apart from the indwelling Holy Spirit will always come up short. The "new birth" is essential to one's progressive understanding of the Bible. Even then, no believer has ever mastered the eternal vastness of God's eternal Word. So, one must keep on reading daily, while praying with David, "Open thou mine eyes [spiritual] that I may behold wondrous things out of thy law [Word]." (Ps. 119:18)

I illustrate the above thought by citing the young secretary who was given a book written by her boss. She tried reading a chapter or two, but soon became disinterested and put it away. Sometime later, she and the boss were married; eventually she picked up her husband's book and read it with intense interest and understanding. What made the difference? She was now married to the author, and that intimate relationship cause the husband's writings to come alive in her soul! So it is when one is in a "saving (living) relationship" with the God of the Word—It (the Word) comes alive!

Since we're exhorted to "study" this Word diligently and correctly, we have no small challenge. I mention again that Paul exhorts young Timothy to "study to show thyself approved unto God, a workman that needeth not to be ashamed, *rightly dividing* the word of truth" (2 Tim. 2:15, italics mine). This verse depicts the pastor as a dead-serious student, diligently seeking to properly and accurately interpret God's Word; this entails being a "workman," one who literally "expends" mental and spiritual energy to correctly understand and convey God's mind and purpose in the intended Scripture. The word for "rightly dividing" is *orthotoméō,* basically meaning "to make a straight cut, i.e. (figuratively) to dissect (expound) correctly (the divine message):—rightly divide."   To fail here is to bring "shame" and untold harm to ourselves and those we teach; not to mention God's disapproval. Significantly, Paul "nails" this concept to Timothy's heart in 1 Timothy 4:13-16:

> Till I come, give attendance to reading, to exhortation, to doctrine. Neglect not the gift that is in thee... Meditate upon these things; give thyself wholly to them; that thy profiting may appear to all. Take heed unto thyself, and unto the doctrine; continue in them: for in doing this thou shalt both *save thyself, and them that hear thee.* (emphasis mine)

Since the Holy Spirit is the Chief-Editor of the Scriptures, walking obediently in His fullness is essential to a right understanding of what He has written; moreover, to "meditate day and night" on God's Word is to facilitate fellowship (spiritual intimacy) with the Spirit of Truth! With that thought in mind, what greater incentive do we need to be "sold out" to God; especially in light of Christ's Return? (cf. 1 John. 2:28-3:3) No one can calculate the damage done by those who willfully and/or ignorantly have "wrongly" divided the Scriptures; thus, as a preacher, I must "save myself" before I can "save others;" i.e. I can't lead others any further than I have gone.

I will be the first to admit that I've missed the true meaning of many Scriptures over years of ministry, including much of what I address in this book. I regret my ignorance, but am grateful for many obscure passages that have become increasingly clear as I've grown in grace and the knowledge of Christ (2 Pet. 3:18). This has challenged me to be saturated with the Word so as to better understand (interpret) the mind of the Living Word. (cf. 1 Cor. 2:9-12) It must be said that how we treat the Written Word is how we treat the Living Word!

Rules of Interpretation

In my research for "Rules of Interpretation," I was inundated with more material than I could digest. Many valuable books are written on the subject for those interested in further study. For the purpose of this book, I want to share some basic precepts on how to "rightly divide (understand) the Word..." These are in question form, and are absolutely essential to accurate interpretation of Truth. (adapted from Thomas Taylor's Bible Hermeneutics).

Here are vital questions to ask about the Bible passage to be interpreted:

Who is speaking?

Who is being spoken to?

When did it happen?

What is the main theme?

What is being said?

The foremost "rule" attached to these questions pertains to **context. context. context!** It is disconcerting to hear preaching and teaching that totally disregards the matter of **context**. For instance, Prov. 11:30 states that "...he that winneth souls is wise." How often I've heard that text used in a "soul-winning"

33

clinic to promote personal evangelism. In context, I doubt that King Solomon was passing out Gospel tracts in front of the palace; nor was he "button-holing" (pressuring) people to "get saved." Obviously we cannot "save" anyone. The verse does teach, however, that through godly living we can expect to "win" the hearts and friendship of others. By application, we can say that as we "win" folks to ourselves, hopefully, this personal witness will "set the stage" for God to "save" them. Someone said, "We must be win-some to win some!"

No Scripture passage ever stands alone. Every Scripture must be read within the context (setting) of the passage in which it is found, while keeping the whole Bible in mind. Beloved, this is probably the most violated rule among us, and yet the most important one. It's been said that if the passage in context makes sense, why look for any other sense? For years, holding a basic covenant position, I spiritualized or allegorized much of the Old Testament to make it "line up" with a New Testament concept; e.g. seeing the Cross in certain trees, and the Holy Spirit in some rain cloud or vial of oil, etc. The Old Testament stands alone, with its legitimate types of Christ (e.g. Joseph, Moses, David, etc.), along with myriads of applications; but its content must never be spiritually "forced" to fit into the New. Both Testaments are progressively revealed in their own right; they cannot be contextually "homogenized." Not to be facetious, but it could be said of one now-deceased "hyper-covenant" teacher that he could find the "gospel" in an ant crawling up the backside of a horse! That's not a compliment. Let us exercise great care in accurately and reverently interpreting God's Holy Word.

When receiving an important document or letter by certified mail, we take great care to read it thoroughly. Because of its serious nature, we dare not "extract" independent statements here and there; rather, we make sure that each sentence and/or paragraph is understood in the context of the author's intent. To misinterpret parts of this weighty document could foster misunderstanding and erroneous conclusions. Such could prove to be embarrassing and costly. How much more is this true with our treatment of Holy Scripture?

It's essential that the Bible should be understood in its normal, clear, regular sense of meaning, considering carefully its context or setting; i.e. the text must be taken at face value. I repeat the maxim that "When the plain sense of Scripture makes sense, seek no other sense;" therefore consider each word in its primary, grammatical, ordinary meaning unless "the facts of the immediate context, studied in light of related passages and axiomatic and fundamental truths, indicate clearly otherwise." We do not have liberty to simply allegorize or spiritualize portions of Scripture that we don't understand or do not fit into our theological framework.

For many years I made little distinction between the Old and New Testaments (Covenants); I saw the Bible as basically "one volume" revealing God's plan for man's personal redemption, which certainly is true; however, I became aware of how little interest I had in the prophetic passages written by the Old Testament prophets. I was led to believe that all those prophesies found their fulfillment in the church, *not* referring to Israel's future, literal restoration on earth (Millennium); thus, with national Israel now off the scene, the Christian becomes a member of "spiritual Israel" (church); and those prophetic utterances regarding Israel's future simply depict the coming glory of the Church triumphant. This is a blessed thought, but does it fit the context of the whole Bible? Is it "rightly dividing" Scripture, especially in light of Paul's account of Israel's future in Romans 9-11?

CHAPTER 4

UNDERSTANDING GOD'S PROGRESSIVE REVELATION

We must also understand that God's Word (the Bible) is progressive by design. God unfolds His revelation down through history in a progressive manner. For instance, Salvation is revealed from Genesis to Revelation through the necessity of blood sacrifice. The first couple was covered with an animal skin, replacing their fig-leaves (Gen. 3:21). Obviously that skin covering came as a result of taking the life's blood of an innocent animal. Noah, Abraham, Jacob, etc. offered up blood sacrifices to God by faith. The Passover was given to Moses whereby an innocent lamb was offered for the sins of the people. After the Law or Ten Commandments were given in forming a Theocratic (God-ruled) nation, the breaking of those commands demanded sacrificial blood to atone or cover personal sin (cf. Ex. 12; Lev. 16, etc.)

Israel continued this practice throughout its 1500 year history until Messiah came as "the Lamb who taketh away the sin of the world." (John 1:29) No more daily sacrifice of innocent animals, for now The Lamb **Himself** had come to fulfill the Law completely, giving the ultimate, once-for-all Sacrifice for sinners! Hallelujah!

Quality vs Quantity

God's revelation is like a progression from the "seed" in Genesis, to the "sapling", (Gospels), and then the "full bloomed tree" in Revelation. The Lord Himself has never changed, for He is "the same yesterday, today and forever;" likewise, the *quality* (essence) of His salvation has never changed throughout human history; but the *quantity* (increase, amount) of His revelation has progressed or advanced over time. For example,

King Solomon was just as "saved" as believers today; i.e. by faith in the God-ordained blood sacrifice. But unlike the present-day believer, he had to offer a spotless lamb at the Temple. Thankfully, our Sacrificial Lamb has been already offered *once-for-all and forever!* (cf. Heb. 9:19-28) We may have more revelation than Solomon because we have the whole Bible; but his obedient faith in God's provision for sin is no different than ours. In any age, faith is simply taking God at His word. The program or agenda may progressively change, but the same unchanging God reigns Supreme. He faithfully dispenses and unfolds His perfect plan without ever contradicting or compromising His immutable (absolute, unchanging) character.

Word Meanings and Doctrine

Another essential ingredient in proper interpretation is meaning or definition of words. Since we believe in the "verbal, plenary (full) Inspiration" of Scripture; i.e. every single word of the Old and New Testament (in the original manuscripts) is "God-breathed" (2 Tim. 3:16&17). Every "word" is from God Himself! How that should enthrall and motivate us to exhaust the meaning of each word (in its context or setting). As mentioned above, God gave this Revelation (The Bible) through holy men who spoke the Word as they were borne (lit. carried) along by the Holy Spirit. (cf. 2 Pet. 1:20, 21)

Therefore, let us diligently ask: "What does the word mean?" We should never be glib or casual in reading Scripture, knowing the human authors spoke from God with words full of purpose and meaning.. *Remember, the meaning is determined by the author, and discovered by the readers.* We have an obligation to find the plain meaning of these words, reading *out (exegesis)* from the passage, rather than "reading into" it *(eisogesis)*.

This is where the Historic and Grammatical usage of language comes into play; this is God's infallible Word, demanding careful research in its original language and setting. Every preacher/teacher should have at least a working (practical) understanding of Biblical Hebrew and Greek. Significantly, Paul commends the Berean Christians for being "more noble" than others, "in that they received the word with all readiness of mind, and searched the Scriptures daily, whether these things were so." (cf. Acts 17:10-12) There's room today for some serious and diligent "searching" for what the Bible says, as well as what it *doesn't* say!

Over the past few decades, I have witnessed a decrease of doctrinal teaching, catechism classes, and even Sunday schools. It was not uncommon, particularly in Presbyterian and Lutheran churches, to disciple children in the Word, using the Westminster Confession of Faith, for instance. The Fundamentalist Movement of the 1920s was an attempt to counter the plague of anti-Biblical Modernism in the Church. Men, like Dr. J. Gresham Machen, and other Princeton graduates, headed the so-called Fundamentalist-Modernist Controversy. There was great emphasis on teaching children and adults the basic doctrines of Scripture on a continuing weekly basis. As imperfect as these movements were, they helped stem the tide of the raging satanic attacks on the infallibility of the Bible.

CHAPTER 5
THE EFFECTS OF SPIRITUAL AWAKENINGS

Modern Church history is replete with some mighty moves of God which greatly affected American Christianity. The Methodist Camp Meeting Revival (1800) and the New York Fulton Street revival (1856) were greatly used to extend the ministry of the Church. By the late 19th Century, Churches in America were already spiritually linked to those in Britain through the ministry of men like Charles Spurgeon (London) and D.L. Moody (Chicago). These movements were preparatory for one of the most extensive and phenomenal outpourings of the Holy Spirit; i.e. the so-called Welsh Revival of 1904. Beginning in Wales, this awakening not only permeated the British Isles, but spread rapidly across the Atlantic to the States. Churches were spiritually stirred and transformed, resulting in multitudes of people coming to Jesus Christ.

New denominations were formed through men like A.B. Simpson, a Presbyterian minister who wanted to promote Spirit-filled missions; thus, the Christian and Missionary Alliance was born. At the same time, the Pentecostal movement gained impetus through a corresponding revival called the Azusa Street Prayer Meeting (1906). The human instrument was William J. Seymour, a one-eyed, African-American Holiness preacher, who had come to Los Angeles seeking a pastoral job. Facing opposition, he began a prayer meeting in a home where God began to "pour out His Spirit;" Seymour called this the "Second blessing," while others referred to this experience as the "Baptism of power." Also called "The Baptism in the Holy Ghost," this teaching became the "bench mark" for true "Spirit-filled" believers; simply put, one had to return to Acts 2:4 (Pentecost) and receive the "gift of the Holy Ghost" with evidence of "speaking in an unknown tongue." This teaching became a primary distinction in the eventual worldwide growth of the Pentecostal and Charismatic movements.

The Great Awakening

This revival in Wales was preceded by the so-called Great Awakening of 1730 under Jonathan Edwards that shook New England to the core. Edwards' famous sermon, "Sinners in the Hands of an Angry God," left parishioners clutching the pews and/or falling to the floor under deep conviction of sin. Multitudes were converted to Christ and "Eternity" became the ongoing topic of discussion on New England streets.

In light of our discussion on the "Power of Pentecost," the reader is encouraged to study Jonathan Edwards' life and ministry. He is acclaimed as probably the greatest and most profound theologian in American history. The great Scottish preacher, Thomas Chalmers, wrote, "Never was there a happier combination of great power with great piety." But underneath Edwards' "experiential theology" was his bed-rock foundation and understanding of Holy Scripture. It's said, that "for Edwards, Biblical exposition was the soul, sinew, and marrow of his life and purpose."

Fortunately, or unfortunately, "revivals" come to an end. While churches are awakened and souls are "swept" into the Kingdom during these times, the lasting effect is short-lived. That being said, the ongoing fruit and advancement of the Church through these spiritual awakenings must not be minimized. Despite the fleshly outbursts, and even demonic activity, it demonstrates how God uses imperfect people to advance His divine agenda. To put it another way, "God can use a crooked stick to draw a straight line."

Experience Begins to Override Sound Doctrine

The mainline denominations, like Presbyterians, Lutherans, Episcopalians, etc. have increasingly become more "liberal," moving away from the inspiration and ultimate authority of the Bible. This has produced what is commonly called the Ecumenical Movement, emphasizing social and religious unity; the bedrock doctrines of the Blood Atonement of Christ, His Virgin Birth, Bodily Resurrection, the need to be "born again," etc. began to wane in importance. There was an increasing exodus from these large denominations, spawning a number of smaller churches who still embraced the afore-mentioned "fundamentals" of the Faith.

Interestingly, along with this ecumenical movement came an increased interest in the "gifts of the Holy Spirit," particularly "healing and speaking in tongues." As previously mentioned, the so-called "Baptism of the Holy Ghost" evidenced by "speaking in other tongues" (Acts 2:4) became the benchmark in determining if a believer was "filled with the Holy Spirit."

Certain denominations, like the Assembly of God, have always held this teaching, but now the "experience" began to go main-stream. This became part of the so-called "renewal" in the ecumenical Episcopalian Church. In 1960, Fr. Dennis Bennett, an Episcopalian rector in Van Nuys, CA, is said to have initiated this movement. His professed experience of "speaking in tongues" was unheard of among Episcopalians; but this "phenomenon" was eventually embraced by others and eventually spread to other main-line denominations.

Gifts Used to Fuel Ecumenical Apostasy

This implemented another "phenomenon" whereby those who continued to deny the fundamentals of Biblical Christianity could now "unify" and "fellowship" around "spiritual gifts." Eventually historic Protestant churches were linking up with

Roman Catholicism, finding common ground primarily through the gifts of tongues and healing. The 16th Century Protestant Reformation, previously denouncing the doctrinal heresies of Romanism, was now being "bridged" together by means of these "spiritual gifts." What a clever scheme of the Enemy to further promote one-world, ecumenical church apostasy!

In recent years, a group of well-known Charismatic leaders met with the Pope of Rome to declare their unity with the "True Church," which illustrates the trend to override doctrinal purity and authority with so-called "experiential" unity. Supposedly, Protestants ("evangelicals") and Catholics can now unite on the so-called "Spirit's baptism;" thus overriding or nullifying the age-old doctrinal warfare regarding "salvation by faith *alone*, through Christ *alone*. True Christianity has been established on the infallibility and Divine inspiration of the Holy Scriptures (the Bible) as the Hallmark of faith and practice. The Holy Spirit is the Chief Editor of the Bible; thus, He is the Spirit of Truth, never contradicting the Word of Truth! To talk of being "filled with the Holy Spirit," while denying Biblical inerrancy and salvation by grace alone (apart from good works) is nothing short of blasphemy.

In other words, my "experience in the Holy Ghost" is valid even if I reject the infallibility and final authority of the Scripture (Bible), which was given by the same Holy Spirit! This scenario has been a very effective ploy of Satan to help bring a mixed multitude together in the formation of his (Satan's) one-world religion. (cf. Ex. 12:38; Neh. 13:3) What couldn't be accomplished on a strict Biblical (doctrinal) base is being spawned through an undue emphasis on subjective experience.

The Holy Spirit never contradicts or leads anyone contrary to the Word He has given! He alone has come to reveal the Living Christ and the Savior's teaching; in fact, the Spirit never "speaks of Himself," but His focus is *always* on the Lord Jesus

Christ! (cf. John 14:26; 16:12-15) If the so-called "gifts of the Spirit" do not point to (exalt) Jesus Christ, then they are *not* motivated by the Holy Spirit! The early church was "invaded" by the Holy Spirit of Christ so that Christ might be seen and glorified. Since the Gospel is defined as the "death, burial, and resurrection of Christ (1 Cor. 15:3&4), then the Spirit-filled believer will be totally enraptured by and focused on the living Savior.

Likewise, someone who is filled with the Holy Spirit will be filled with the Word of Truth. (cf. Eph. 5:18f & Col. 3:16f) Those who profess to be "filled with the Spirit" need to be challenged on the Scriptural veracity of their so-called "experience." We ought never to judge the Bible by what we "feel," but rather we must check out our "feelings" by the Bible! The apostate movement in Christendom has dared to claim unity and brotherhood on the basis of "spiritual experience," which is untenable and without Biblical authority.

Jesus clarified this issue to a newly converted Samaritan woman who desired to be a "true worshipper" of Jehovah. (cf. John 4:21-26) After exposing her lifeless, religious traditions, he tells her that "true worshippers shall worship the Father *in spirit and in truth*...God is a Spirit; and they that worship him must worship him *in spirit and in truth*." (vs. 23-24; emphasis mine) Worship has to do with "worthiness," thus, "worth-ship." Since our God is "altogether worthy," we worship (venerate) Him alone! The Spirit has revealed Him as the Truth in the Word of Truth (Scripture); but that knowledge is only understood in the "spirit" (heart) of the believer, illumined by the Holy Spirit. True worship must comprise the balance of truth (Word) *and* spiritual (heart) engagement. Some folks seem to have truth with little "spirit;" while others seem to manifest "spirit" with little truth.

This imbalance has produced no small problem in the Church. True Spirit-filled worship must have a balance of "spirit and truth;" but "spirit" worship is not to be relegated solely to outward emotion; it flows much deeper. I've said for years that if you have truth without spirit, you will "dry up;" if you have spirit without truth, you will "blow up;" but if you have truth *and* spirit, you will "grow up!" O, for an "epidemic" of this divine balance in the church where true "worshippers" manifest Christ in both "head and heart!" (cf. 2 Pet. 3:18)

CHAPTER 6

PENTECOST AND MY PERSONAL JOURNEY

For over 60 years, I have labored in the Scriptures to find the mind of God for my life and ministry. Few subjects have taken more of that time than the meaning and purpose of Pentecost (Acts. 1&2). As a very young preacher, I wrestled with the reality of Acts 1:8: "But ye shall receive power, after that the Holy Ghost is come upon you: and ye shall be witnesses unto me both in Jerusalem, and in all Judaea, and in Samaria, and unto the uttermost part of the earth."

I devoured books and sermons on the "power of Pentecost" and knew that I could not settle for anything less. I found that commentators differed and even "bickered" over what this "power" was and how it was obtained. But whatever it was, they all agreed that it was essential to have. A Southern preacher was once asked to define the "unction (power) of the Holy Ghost;" he replied, "I don't knows what it is, but I sure knows what it ain't!"

The Holy Spirit's power is a reality that defies explanation. One of my mentors likened the Spirit's unction to a new-born baby. You may not know what to call the baby, but that doesn't change the baby's existence. To have a name for the baby is far less important than the reality of having the baby! The point is, we need to have the "baby" whether we know what to call it or not! I came to a place in my life that I must have that "baby;" i.e. the "power of God" to permeate my entire being.

Encounter with the Holy Spirit

I remember distinctly the day that I wrestled with the Lord over this matter of being "filled" with the Spirit; after considerable struggle, I finally cried out to God in faith that He would bless me with the reality of the Spirit's "divine power." Yes, I made a definite appropriation (receiving) of His provision, and the change was evident. A whole new vista of understanding and effectiveness opened; the Word became more alive and meaningful. I began to realize how that my experience correlated with Paul's exhortation in Eph. 5:18, to "not be drunk with wine...but *be filled* with the Holy Spirit." I eventually understood that this "encounter" with the Holy Spirit was meant to be an ongoing reality or life-style. It has been referred to as "the Normal Christian life," made possible by the Spirit's "invasion" at Pentecost!

Over the years there has been some misunderstanding regarding the manifestation of the Holy Sprit's coming. Symbols like water, wind, fire, and anointing oil, etc. have been used to depict His ministry. First and foremost, however, He is a *person*; i.e. the Third Person of the Trinity, who Himself dwells in every believer. (cf. 1 Cor. 6:19) For instance, when we pray, "fill my cup, Lord," it infers that we need "more" of the Spirit; in reality, that's a figure of speech expressing our desire for the Spirit to take "full charge" of our lives. We have "all of Him" from the beginning of salvation, but the ongoing issue in our Christian walk is "does He have *all of us*?"

Interestingly, a baby is born fully "equipment" up front. His body parts are all in tact even though he's basically ignorant of their function(s). After a time, for instance, he lifts his hand in the crib, watching and wondering what it is. Eventually, he discovers its use and purpose, which develops over time. God didn't "attach" that hand when he needed it, but *before* he ever used it! So our Heavenly Father has "equipped" us from the very start of salvation; we are indwelt ("baptized") by the Holy Spirit right up front, even though we progressively discover how to appropriate His full provision for godly living. Salvation is an ongoing "enterprise" led and empowered by the Spirit of Pentecost!

Are "Filling" and "Fullness" the Same?

As a young grad student, one of my mentors dropped a seed thought that has slowly "germinated" over the years. He posed the question as to the possible distinction between the "filling" and the "fullness" of the Holy Spirit. I think that present-day confusion warrants such a clarification.

The Old Testament is replete with examples of God's servants being empowered by His Spirit to fulfill a particular task. In the book of Judges, the term "the Spirit of the LORD came upon him" is used to express God's unction upon men like, Gideon (6:34); Jephthah (11:29); and Sampson (14:6, 19; 15:14). These leaders were mightily endued with the Spirit's power to deliver Israel from enemy oppression. The same term is used of Saul's anointing as king by Samuel, who says, "The Spirit of the LORD shall come upon thee and thou shalt…be turned into another man." (1Sam. 10:6)

In the case of King David's inauguration, it says that "Samuel took the horn of oil, and anointed him in the midst of his brethren: and the Spirit of the LORD came upon David from that day forward." (1Sam. 16:13) Sometime later, David testifies that "The Spirit of the LORD spake by me, and his word was in my tongue," thus revealing his contribution as an inspired writer of Holy Scripture. (1Sam. 23:2; Ps. 45:1; 2 Pet.1:20, 21)

This same expression of the Spirit's ministry is further used in Isa. 11:2 to describe the seven-fold (fullness) of God's Spirit upon Israel's Messiah: *"The spirit of the LORD shall rest upon him, the spirit of wisdom and understanding, the spirit of counsel and might, etc."* John the Baptist is recorded as an eyewitness of this fulfillment saying,

I saw the Spirit descending from heaven like a dove, and it abode upon him. And I knew him not: but he that sent me to baptize with water, the same said unto me, *upon whom thou shalt see the Spirit descending, and remaining on him,* the same is he which baptizeth with the Holy Ghost. (John 1:32, 33; emphasis mine)

In Old Testament times, God's "Spirit moved upon" His servants in a transitory manner (e.g. Midian, Sampson, Elijah); but now the Spirit descends and *remains* permanently upon Jesus Christ. After all, He (Jesus), unlike anyone else, possessed the Spirit without measure or limit. (cf. John. 3:34)
This leads us to that monumental prophecy in Isaiah 61:1f from which Jesus confronts the Jews in the synagogue of Nazareth after His "bout" with Satan. (cf. Lk. 4:13ff). The Prophet Isaiah records the words of Messiah thusly:

> *The Spirit of the Lord GOD is upon me*; because the LORD hath *anointed me* to preach good tidings unto the meek; he hath sent me to bind up the brokenhearted, to proclaim liberty to the captives, and the opening of the prison to them that are bound. (Isa. 61:1; emphasis mine)

In this context, Luke depicts Jesus as "being full of the Holy Ghost" as He is about to be tempted of the devil. (Lk. 4:1) More than an "anointing" here, this term "being full" (adj., *pleres*) speaks to His [Jesus'] condition or state, rather than a mere action. Not to split hairs, but this term "full of the Holy Ghost" is used only of Jesus until after Pentecost; in Acts 6:3, only men "full of the Holy Ghost" could qualify for the deacon's office. The same is said of Stephen in Acts. 7:55 and Barnabas in Acts 11:24. This ties directly to Eph. 5:18, "and be not drunk with wine, wherein is excess; but be filled [lit. be being full] with the Spirit."

This is a present passive imperative (command) from *pleroo*, describing a saint being "filled up to capacity" with the One who dwells within. The present tense indicates an ongoing condition resulting from the Holy Spirit's initial work of sanctification or salvation (cf. 1 Cor. 1:30; 12:13). There's no going back to Pentecost here but rather living in the present reality of the Holy Spirit's once-for-all indwelling, sealing, and baptism into the Body of Christ. (cf. 1 Cor. 3:16; Eph. 1:7; 1 Cor. 12:13)

The progression of revelation through Paul clarifies our position in Christ, and the blessed ministry of the Holy Spirit. Paul tells us "let the word of Christ dwell in you richly..." (Col. 3:16) Just as the Spirit dwells within us, so does the Word; thus we "let" it happen, there's no "stirring the religious pot" or looking for a new "experience." We are to "work out" (not work *up*) our salvation with fear and trembling; because it is God who "works in us both to will and to do of His good pleasure." (Phil. 2:12, 13) We can't work out something that we don't already possess; so with a yielded heart, we "work out" what God is "working in!" That's an ongoing enterprise established and made available at Pentecost.

Mysterious Work of the Spirit in Regeneration

Similarly, Jesus told Nicodemus that "except a man be born again, he cannot see the kingdom of God." (John 3:3) The term "born again" literally means a "birth from on high" (*anothen*- used in vs.31) as opposed to a natural birth in the flesh. Nicodemus quickly reveals his ignorance of the subject, as Jesus likens this "new birth" of the Spirit to the sovereign, invisible blowing of the wind. (vss. 6-8) Jesus insists that "Ye (all Israel) must be born again," yet with no instructions as to "how." Nowhere are we told "to get borned again", as some preachers say; it's rather a mysterious work of the Holy Spirit moving upon a darkened soul as He did in the first creation (cf. Gen. 1:2). Paul states that the "God who commanded the light to shine out of darkness, hath shined in our hearts to give the light of the knowledge…of Jesus Christ" (2 Cor.4:6). Could this not be illustrated by Lydia's experience in Acts 16:14? She's described by Luke as one *"whose heart the Lord opened* [so] that she attended unto the things which were spoken of Paul?" (italics mine)

My point is that as believers we need not "seek the Holy Ghost" per se, but by faith receive, enjoy, and depend upon the Spirit of Christ within. We must live in the overflow from the outflow of our heavenly Intercessor who, according to Jesus, would live in us forever! Amen.

CHAPTER 7
THE "FULL GOSPEL"

The evidences of spiritual awakening were many during my first pastorate in So. Canaan, PA. In five years of ministry (1963-68) we witnessed a marvelous move of converting grace and the reviving of a church ministry that had been struggling for years. A godly man, Pastor Ralph Lucy, labored faithfully there for 39 years before retiring. He was directly instrumental in my coming, and faithfully encouraged me by prayer and correspondence in my new venture. What happened there was classic, and really too sacred to recount in detail. Suffice it to say that many were genuinely saved and are still stalwart in the Faith to this day. Some serve with their families in the local church, while others have been planted on other mission fields. The church continues to thrive in a tiny community, graduating a steady stream of students from its Academy who are impacting the world. It's been undoubtedly the closest example of true, Holy Spirit revival and reformation that I've ever witnessed.

Hungry for God's Best

During those early days, I rubbed shoulders with all kinds of Christians, having a desire to love the brethren and be further edified. On one occasion, a dear lady invited me to attend a "healing" crusade at a local Pentecostal church. I consented to go, and was placed right up front where I could watch all the proceedings. I don't remember the sermon, but afterward a number of people came forward to get their "legs lengthened." I watched with some skepticism, while trying to be "open" to God's working. I figured if this "healing" helped folks to "walk the walk for Jesus," (no pun intended) it seemed good to me! I left that meeting with an uneasy spirit, questioning the veracity of what I witnessed. If there were genuine "healings," the word never got out.

Interestingly, however, it was several years later, that a newer pastor of that church committed suicide. I'm only inferring that "healing ministry" per se is not a "catch all" or panacea. Because a minister preaches the so-called "full Gospel" doesn't mean he's "arrived" at the pinnacle of Holy Ghost power. The cocky attitude that permeates so much of this movement is the height of spiritual arrogance and pride. "Let him that thinketh he standeth, take heed lest he fall."

Some have probably questioned why I would even attend such a meeting. Let me say that as a young fledging pastor I was hungry for God's best, and eager to learn from others. I wanted to be all that I could be for God's glory, and was even open to "speaking in tongues" if that was part of the equation. I wanted every Biblically legitimate blessing that God had to offer me so that I might be "thoroughly furnished" (equipped) to serve Him. In fact, I was all but defrocked from the denomination I served for denying that certain gifts of the Spirit were passé. I'm saying that I've been open to God's truth, regardless of the approval or disapproval of others.

Why "Full Gospel"?

Sometime later, I heard of the Full Gospel Business Men's group that was forming in the area. I had only known of the Christian Business Men's Association, which had similar objectives. I was curious as to why the necessity of these two groups? After some inquiry, I found out that the former group was geared for those who believed not only in being spiritually "born again" per se, but additionally embraced complete physical healing now through Christ's atonement, along with the so-called "baptism in the Spirit" with evidence of "speaking in tongues;" thus the label "Full Gospel," inferring that apart from the outward witness of certain "gifts" the salvation experience was "incomplete." Fortunately (or unfortunately) this placed a doctrinal "wedge" between Christian businessmen who were Charismatic; i.e. the "haves," and the other group who were non-Charismatic, the "have nots."

Initially, I had no problem with the "full Gospel" terminology, since I knew that Christ is my "Healer." There's no way a believer, or anyone, can live for a moment without His healing power. In fact, medical science has indicated that our body cells are generally renewed (regenerated) every seven to fifteen years. So what's wrong with "full Gospel" since God is healing the whole man!

But then I began checking the proof-texts being used to support "healing in the atonement." Isaiah 53: 5ff speaks of the "Suffering Servant," Israel's Messiah coming the first time to "bear the sins of many." "He was wounded for our transgressions; he was bruised for our iniquities, and by his stripes we are healed." This is a clear picture of Jesus Christ taking the judgment of God's wrath for the sins of His people. Peter clearly verifies Isaiah's prophetic word and intent in 1 Pet. 2:23- 25:

> Who, when he [Jesus] was reviled, reviled not again; when he suffered, he threatened not; but committed himself to him that judgeth righteously; *Who his own self bare our sins in his own body on the tree, that we, being dead to sins, should live unto righteousness; by whose stripes ye were healed.* For ye were as sheep going astray; but are now returned unto the Shepherd and Bishop of your souls. (italics mine)

Distinguishing Sin from Sickness

Anyone reading the above passage honestly and with no bias, will conclude that the prophet's words refer specifically and primarily to Messiah's substitutionary Blood Sacrifice and

Atonement for *sin.* Certainly physical healing is ultimately inclusive, but to use this as a "proof text" to claim bodily healing as you would forgiveness, is bogus; especially since God was healing folks way before Calvary. Saving faith or spiritual healing is instantaneous and complete in Christ. (cf. Rom.3:21-26; 4:3-5; 8:1) The body or fleshly tabernacle in which we live is dying and groaning along with the rest of creation; we are awaiting the Lord's Coming to be "delivered from the bondage of corruption into the glorious liberty of the children of God...the redemption of the body." (Rom. 8:21, 23)

Paul exhorts us to anticipate Christ's Return from Heaven when He will "change our vile body that it may be fashioned like unto his glorious body..." (Phil. 3:20, 21) Certainly, there is an ongoing ministry of divine healings as we journey through this life time, but they are temporary at best. The ultimate permanent healing or "clothing upon" is yet to come. The apostle beautifully describes this event thusly:

> For we know that if our earthly house of this tabernacle [lit. tent] were dissolved, we have a building of God, an house not made with hands, eternal in the heavens. For in this we groan, earnestly desiring to be clothed upon with our house which is from heaven: If so be that being clothed we shall not be found naked. For we that are in this tabernacle [body] do groan, being burdened: not for that we would be unclothed, but clothed upon, that mortality might be swallowed up of life...We are confident, I say, and willing rather to be absent from the body, and to be present with the Lord. (2 Cor. 5:1-4,8; cf. 1 Cor. 15:34ff)

It's obvious that true believers are dying physically; i.e. the "outward man is perishing...yet the inward man is renewed day by day" (2 Cor.4:16). He (the believer) is dying and living at the same time! Regenerated and sealed by the Holy Spirit within (Eph. 1:13), yet his flesh (tent) is headed for the grave. That tells me that our spirit (heart) is saved *now*, but the "redemption" of the body is yet future. (cf. Rom. 8:16-23) I've often wondered why God didn't give us a "new body" at the time of our spiritual salvation. That would have settled a lot of arguments.

Therefore we cannot place physical healing on the same level as the atonement for sin. If sin and sickness are equivalent then everyone will end up in Hell, seeing that, if Jesus tarries, we'll all die of something! I trust we would agree that true believers who die with a dreaded disease go to Heaven, while sinners who die of "natural causes" are still lost forever. That being said, our God's healing power has in no way been diminished in our day; but the primary emphasis of the Cross is the once-for-all payment for man's sin, bringing eternal salvation and forgiveness to his soul!

Paul's "Thorn"

After his conversion to Christ, Paul was "caught up to the third heaven," receiving directly from the Lord "unspeakable words...not lawful for a man to utter." (2 Cor. 12:2, 4) He goes on to relate how God moved to prevent Paul's pride and self-"exaltation." He says,

> And lest I should be exalted above measure through the abundance of the revelations, there was given to me a thorn in the flesh, the messenger of Satan to buffet me, lest I should be exalted above measure. For this thing I besought the Lord thrice, that it might depart from me. And he said unto me, *My grace is sufficient for thee: for my strength is made perfect in weakness.* Most gladly therefore will I rather

> glory in my infirmities, that the power of Christ
> may rest upon me. (2 Cor. 12:7-9; italics mine)

God knows how to train and deal with His servants, using whatever means necessary.(cf. Heb. 12:5&6) It may "wrinkle" our theology, but the Lord clearly used Satan to perfect Job; could this not explain Paul's "thorn" as some kind of ongoing physical and/or emotional trauma instigated by Satan, yet under God's control? Whatever the case, the apostle's "thorn in the flesh" (cf. 2 Cor. 12:1-9) was not removed (healed) due to God's particular purpose in "afflicting" His apostle. It was God's way of keeping Paul humble and useful in light of the Lord's marvelous revelation of the Gospel of "the dispensation of the grace of God..." (cf. Eph. 3:1-14; 1 Cor. 15:1-4; 2 Cor. 12:2-9)

We can see from this passage that this seeming "unanswered prayer" had nothing to do with God's inability to heal or Paul's lack of faith. It was rather God's divine strategy (and prerogative) to keep His servant in line. We're not told how long he had the "thorn" but undoubtedly Paul found the "grace of God sufficient." I have to believe that Church History is replete with similar episodes yet to be revealed in Heaven. (e.g. Heb. 11)

Jesus' Miracles Comfort John in Prison

Christ's forerunner, John the Baptist, preached the Kingdom message without performing miracles; he ended up in jail, soon to be beheaded. Hearing from prison the "works of Christ," he sends word to Jesus asking, "art thou he that should come, or do we look for another?" (Matt. 11:3) Picture John's despairing mental condition, being isolated from the "action" and fellowship of the Twelve. Jesus answers, saying to them:

> Go and show John again those things ye do hear
> and see; the blind receive their sight, and the

> lame walk the lepers are cleansed, and deaf hear,
> and the dead are raised up, and the poor have the
> gospel preached to them. And blessed is he,
> whosoever shall not be offended [caused to
> stumble] in me. (Matt. 11:4-6)

These words describing His (Messiah's) miraculous activity
were used to validate His (Jesus') true identity and bolster
John's faith. Imagine John's unique situation; there he is
waning alone on Herod's "death row" in desperate need of
encouragement and reassurance; after all, he was the first man
to hear God's prophetic call in the 400 years of God's silence
between John's appearance and the end of the Old Testament!
Yes, he certainly walked by faith, but Jesus knew that a report
of supernatural events ("sight") was essential to sustain him in
that dark hour.

Healing Used to Authenticate Christ's Forgiveness

Matthew recounts the episode when Jesus being surrounded by
many demon possessed and sick, brought spiritual and physical
healing (cf. 8:16). The writer states that this was a fulfillment of
Isaiah's prophecy: "Himself (Messiah) took our infirmities, and
bare our sicknesses"(8:17). Obviously, physical healing was a
vital aspect of Jesus' earthly ministry which authenticated His
Messiahship. This is in no way a denial of Christ's healing
power, but only to present the purpose of his healing in context.
Remember, the Atonement (Cross) hadn't taken place yet;
however, Christ was already revealing His saving power en
route to Calvary. Certainly, as mentioned above, there is
ultimate "healing in the Atonement," or the believer would
never anticipate a "glorified body" one day. (cf. 1Cor.15:50f)

In the meantime, there is perpetual "healing" sustained by
God's grace, but that's equally true of unbelievers. Moreover,
"miraculous" healings are happening today among the saved
and the lost. God is the "Savior of all men, specially of those

that believe." (1 Tim. 4:10) God loves and cares for His creation; e.g. the sun shines on the "just and the unjust." But those who believe and are recreated in Christ have a unique relationship with the Lord.

Lesson from a Paralyzed Man

Mark's account of the paralyzed man (2:10-12) has really helped me to clarify this issue. You remember how the four men had to lower the sick man down from the roof to get to Jesus because of the crowd. Mark says, "When Jesus saw their faith, he said unto the sick of the palsy, Son, thy sins be forgiven thee." (2:5) What? Wait a minute! The man is "sick," desperately needing a physical touch from Jesus; instead, Jesus "forgives his sin," leaving the man limp in the stretcher! This puzzled the crowd, especially the Scribes in attendance who accused Jesus of "blasphemy" (vs. 7). They may have tolerated His healings, but "forgiving sins" was too much. Yet, forgiveness of sin was primary, being eternal in essence; physical healing is secondary, seeing it is temporary at best. Healing is important, but not priority. As previously stated, sick believers still go to Heaven, but "well" sinners (unbelievers) will go to Hell.

But that was just the point of Christ's emphasis and purpose for coming; i.e. to forgive sinners! (vs.9&10) Yes, the man was healed, but not before Jesus confirmed His Messiahship to the religionists. The physical miracles were signs (demanded by the Jews) to authenticate and verify the fulfillment of Isaiah's prophecy. We can't simply pull these passages out of context and try to insert them into the present-day situation. Bible History is replete with miraculous events within the purposes of God. The absence of such, however, is no indictment of Gods' ability or omnipotence.

For example, Moses's ministry was replete with the miraculous so as to identify his authority from the Lord. The same was true with Elijah and Elisha, but not so with Isaiah and Jeremiah.

How come? Was Isaiah any less "spiritual" or important than Elijah? I mean aren't preachers and "charismatic leaders" judged by how much "Holy Ghost power" is manifested in the meetings? We've made a show of the "flesh" under the guise of the Spirit! This is not just spiritual pride and arrogance, but a complete twisting of Scriptural context and teaching. (cf. 2Peter 3:15&16) Should we anticipate the Spirit's movement as we preach? Of course; but "working" the crowd emotionally and/or "jacking up" the flesh psychologically with mesmerizing "music," etc. is another matter.

"Playing God" Heresy

Let's face it, if the Holy Spirit is doing exactly what He did in Jesus's earthly ministry, then healings would be abundant, including demonic deliverance and raising folks from the dead! This is not to deny the miraculous, but just to say that the present setting is different. It's easy to relegate the lack of "outward" results to "unbelief" when, in reality there are many strong people of faith today. God doesn't work the same way in every place at every given time.

I knew a dear missionary couple, Bob and Bess Butters, who witnessed a phenomenal outpouring of the Holy Spirit in the Congo in the 1950s. Precious souls were "swept" into the Church, lives were transformed through the Gospel of Christ, and all because "God was down." That expression was used for "revival," or the awesome sense of God's presence; The Lord was "opening hearts," as He did with Lydia in Acts 16:14. They were making spiritual "hay" while the Son was "shining." My friend even testified to me that on one occasion he clearly understood a sermon given by a native pastor whose language was foreign to Bob! God will do what He wants to do! Amen!

These things happen in the plan and purposes of God, but no one makes it happen just by "claiming it" or "speaking a word." The attempt to "hold God hostage" by pointing to a Bible verse is preposterous, to say the least! The Lord is Sovereign and His Spirit moves where He wills; no one commands Him, or presumes to "play God!" If we are saved by grace we are "new creatures" in Christ, but will always be part of His creation; we are "sons (heirs) of God" by the "new birth," but Christ alone is **the** Son of God! To teach that a believer has now become a "little Jesus" or *part of the Trinity*, is crossing the line into blatant heresy!

This parallels the attempt of Satan in the Garden to convince Adam and Eve that they could be God (knowing everything) by "eating the forbidden fruit." The Serpent lied to them, and they "fell" for the temptation, disobeying the Lord. Instead of becoming "like God," they were now ungodly sinners; in turn, Adam's disobedience placed the entire human race under the curse of sin and death. (cf. Rom. 5:12) The ministry today seems replete with false teachers who deceitfully confuse godliness with a "god complex;" as Lucifer of old, being "like God" is not their goal, but rather to "replace God!" (cf. Isa. 14:12f). The nature of sin dictates that man is his own "god," whether he's religious or not. Now some "prosperity preachers" teach this heresy using a perverted understanding of the Bible. Tragically, this doctrinal poison is spreading around the world among Biblically illiterate and undiscerning Christians.

CHAPTER 8

WHAT REALLY HAPPENED AT PENTECOST?

All of our previous discussion is linked to the glorious event in Biblical History called Pentecost. It's imperative that we focus anew on what actually happened on that unique Day. The historic reality of Pentecost with its Biblical implications is monumental in understanding the Third Person of the Godhead. Facing this Divine Event in the light of the whole Bible has been revolutionary to me personally. That's not to say that I've received "new revelation," for the Bible is God's complete Revelation to humanity; however, I believe that as the Second Coming approaches, there may just be further illumination on the Revelation. Some things "hard to be understood" may be clearer now than they were centuries ago; e.g. exposure to fulfilled prophesies worldwide via technology, particularly historic events regarding national Israel, etc. I would place the anticipated Rapture of the Church in this category. After wrestling for years with the Biblical validity of Premillennialism and the "Rapture" controversy, my present perspective is much clearer.

In His post-resurrection ministry, Jesus continued to instruct His disciples regarding the coming of the Comforter, the Holy Spirit. They were told not to leave Jerusalem, but to "wait for the promise of the Father...which ye have heard of me." (Acts 1:4) What "promise" was He talking about? In Luke 24:45-49, after reiterating the necessity to proclaim the gospel and witness throughout the world, He says, "Behold, I send the promise of my Father upon you; but tarry ye in the city of Jerusalem until ye be endued with power from on high." (vs. 49)

Jesus then explains that as John "baptized with water," they would soon "be baptized with the Holy Ghost." (Acts 1:5) What did this all mean to this small band of disciples? Significantly, they responded with a question, revealing what was on their mind: "Lord, wilt thou at this time restore again the kingdom to Israel?" (1:6) It's imperative to note here that they were not rebuked by Jesus, seeing that this event was still in the context of Israel's Kingdom and the Messiah's reign on earth. Instead, He exhorts them regarding their lack of knowledge of "the times or the seasons" which are under the Father's authority and control. (1:7)

Pentecost—Jews Only (No Gentiles)

It's essential to understand that those present here were *Jews* only. Just as the "power from on high" was promised to the Jewish disciples in Luke 24:49, so that promise was to be fulfilled here in Acts 1:8 and 2:4. Who are the "ye" in 1:8? They were the Jews that would gather on the "Feast of First Fruits" (Pentecost), a Jewish holiday, which had nothing to do with Gentiles (non-Jews). They were to gather fifty days after Passover to celebrate the first-fruits of the wheat harvest according to Exodus 34:22. Pentecost (Gr. term meaning "fifty") was a Holy Day, which was commemorated by giving "wave sheaf offerings" of the new harvest before their all-sufficient LORD! (cf. Lev/ 23:15-22)

Jesus the Christ is addressing His people (Israel) here, who, according to Old Testament prophecy, were to be "witnesses unto me (Messiah) both in Jerusalem, and in all Judea...and unto the uttermost part of the earth." It was God's intent for His people Israel to ultimately evangelize the whole world, even though His earthly ministry was focused primarily on Israel. (cf. Isa. 42:6&7; 43:8-11). Notice that Jesus commanded the disciples to "go *not* into the way of the Gentiles...but go rather to the lost sheep of the house of Israel...saying the kingdom of heaven is at hand." (Matthew 10:5-7). This was the "kingdom Gospel" which was to usher in Christ's earthly reign. When Israel rejected His Messianic reign, God calls out the Apostle

Paul, who introduces the Gospel of Grace to Jew and Gentile; thus establishing the "Church" (lit. *called out ones*) or the Body of Christ. (cf. Acts 9:15-16; 1 Cor. 3:16-17; 6:19-20; 12:12-13; 15:1-4; Gal. 1:11-17; Eph. 2:8-10; Col. 1:18-22)

Jewish Evangelists?

It's clear that Jehovah chose His people Israel to share His Glory with the whole world. In Exodus 19:5-6 He exhorts:

> If ye will obey my voice indeed, and keep my covenant, then ye shall be a peculiar treasure unto me above all people; for all the earth is mine. And ye shall be unto me a kingdom of priests [mediators], and an holy nation. These are the words which thou shalt speak.

Jehovah further states in Isa. 42:6&7, "I the LORD have called thee in righteousness, and will hold thine hand, and will keep thee, and give thee for a covenant of the people, for *a light of the Gentiles;* To open the blind eyes, to bring out the prisoners from the prison, and them that sit in darkness out of the prison house." (italics mine)

> *Ye are my witnesses* saith the LORD, and my servant whom I have chosen; that ye may know and believe me, and understand that I am he; before me there was no God formed, neither shall there be after me. I, even I, am the LORD; and *beside me there is no saviour.* (Isa. 43:10 &11; italics mine; cf. Acts 1:8)

In Isa. 49:1-7, the prophet addresses the Lord's compassion for the world and the coming Redeemer. In verse 6, Jehovah says, "...It is a light thing that thou shouldest be my servant to raise up the tribes of Jacob, and to restore the preserved of Israel: I will also give thee for a light to the Gentiles, that thou mayest be my salvation unto the end of the earth." The basic thought here is that God's purpose was not simply to "restore" Israel, but under Messiah's redemptive rule, they (Israel) were to bring Jehovah's "salvation" to the entire world. (e.g. John 1:10-12; 3:16)

This mission is further clarified by Luke's narrative in Acts 13:44ff where the Jews in Antioch were "filled with envy" upon hearing Paul and Barnabas proclaim the Gospel of grace to a synagogue packed out with Gentiles on the Sabbath. Paul rebukes these infuriated Jews for their unbelief and disobedience to follow Jehovah's commission to be "a light to the Gentiles," (cf. Isa. 42:6,7; 49:6) They "missed it," and now this converted Jew, called Paul, is picking up the slack. Hear his classic rebuke:

> It was necessary that the word of God should first have been spoken to you: but seeing ye put it from you, and judge yourselves unworthy of everlasting life, lo, we turn to the Gentiles. For so hath the Lord commanded us, saying, I have set thee to be a light of the Gentiles, that thou shouldest be for salvation unto the ends of the earth. And when the Gentiles heard this, they were glad, and glorified the word of the Lord: and as many as were ordained to eternal life believed (Acts. 13:46-48).

Zacharias' Prophesy

This prophetic theme is further advanced by Luke, who records Zacharias' Spirit-filled prophesy regarding the Messianic Kingdom "introduced" by his son John the Baptist. (See Luke 1:67-80) There's no doubt after reading this passage that Zacharias is contemplating the imminent fulfillment of the Abrahamic and Davidic Covenants (cf. Lk.1:69, 73); this was the long-awaited reality of "Heaven on Earth," and John was chosen to "prepare the way of the LORD." What was John to do? He was "to give knowledge of salvation unto his people by the remission of sins...to give light to them that sit in darkness and in the shadow of death; to guide our feet into the way of peace (Lk. 1:77, 79) Sounds like a "Jewish" evangelist to me! (Remember Jonah?)

It's not incidental that the baby Jesus was "circumcised" according to "the law of Moses" and brought to Jerusalem by Mary and Joseph "to present him to the Lord." (cf. Luke 2:21-24) In conjunction, Simeon, a "just and devout" man was there in the temple, "waiting for the consolation of Israel..." (2:25) The Holy Spirit had revealed to him (Simeon) that "he should not see death until he had seen the Lord's Christ." (2:26) When the parents brought the "child Jesus...after the custom of the law...then he (Simeon) took him up in his arms, and blessed God, and said: 'Lord, now lettest thou thy servant depart in peace...for mine eyes have seen thy salvation.'" (Lk. 2: 27-30)

Paul's Conversion

Could it be that Saul of Tarsus (later Paul), a fanatical Jew, further illustrates and enforces this whole concept by virtue of a direct commission by Jesus Himself on the Damascus Road? Luke describes Saul's "sudden" and miraculous conversion to Jesus Christ. Saul, being called by name, cries out, "Who art thou, Lord...what wilt thou have me to do?" The Lord answers, "I am *Jesus* whom thou persecuteth...arise, and go into the city, and it shall be told thee what thou must do." (cf. Acts 9:3-9; emphasis mine)

Arriving in Damascus, Saul is ministered to by a disciple named Ananias, whom Jesus appointed to assist this "new believer." Ananias hesitated, being skeptical and fearful of Saul, who was known as the "believer basher." "But the Lord said unto him, Go thy way, for *he [Saul] is a chosen vessel unto me; to bear my name before the Gentiles*, and kings, and the children of

Israel. For I will show him how great things he must suffer for my name's sake." (Acts 9:15 & 16; italics mine) Paul's commission is further clarified in Acts 13:46-49 and Galatians 2:1-9.

"Jew First"

Growing up in an Orthodox Jewish neighborhood, I was never "evangelized" by a Jew. I was later converted to Christ through a godly pastor who encouraged me to be a good "witness" for Jesus Christ. In my ignorance, I never considered that the Jews had any connection whatever with Christ, even though He was a Jew. All I knew was that He was my Savior and that the whole Bible was written to me, regardless of context. I disregarded "prophecies" (history in advance) as irrelevant, seeing that I denied any valid distinction between Israel and the Church. I glibly read Isa. 9:6 which says, "For *unto us* a child is born, *unto us* a son is given: and the government shall be upon his shoulder..." Many years later it dawned on me that "unto us" was not "us gentiles." Furthermore, the opening sentence of this verse, prophesies both the First and Second Advent of Messiah, with the Church silently, but mystically "sandwiched" in between!

It's important to recognize that "for unto *us*" refers primarily to Israel and not to the Gentiles or the world. Jesus was a Jew, coming to die as Israel's Messiah (Isa. 53). "He came to his own and his own received him not," John 1:11 says. But, thankfully, "as many as received him to them gave he power to become the sons of God!" (1:12) Here was an open door for Gentiles to be saved, just as those wicked Ninevites in Jonah's day. The prophet witnessed this outpouring of saving grace on those Gentiles which "rubbed" his Jewish prejudice the wrong way. Jonah was proto-type of a Jewish "evangelist" who was to proclaim the Name and Glory of Jehovah to the nations.

The Apostle Peter, ministering to dispersed Jewish believers, picks up on this theme in his epistle He calls them

> **"lively [living] stones built up a spiritual house, an holy priesthood to offer up spiritual sacrifices... a chosen generation, a royal priesthood, an holy nation, a peculiar people that ye should shew forth the praises of him who hath called you out of darkness into his marvelous light." (1Pet. 2:5, 9; cf. Isa. 60:1-3; 61:6).**

This passage surely applies to Gentile believers, but only because we've been "grafted into the natural olive tree" (Israel). (cf. Rom. 11:17f); to ignore this distinction between Jew and Gentile in the plan of God will result in a misinterpretation of Pentecost.

Paul, in like manner, exhorts the Ephesian gentile believers:

> Remember that ye...were without Christ, being aliens from the commonwealth of Israel, and strangers of the covenants of promise, having no hope, and without God in the world. *But now* in Christ Jesus ye...are made nigh [near] by the blood of Christ [Messiah]. For he [Christ] is our peace, who hath made both one... (Eph. 2:11-14; emphasis mine)

Simply put, the hopeless gentile sinner had no chance of salvation apart from the Cross-work of Israel's Messiah (Isa. 53; John 3:16)! Significantly, Paul captures this idea when declaring his "gospel of Christ" as the "power of God unto salvation to everyone that believeth; *to the Jew first*, and also to the Greek [Gentile]" (Rom. 1:16; emphasis mine).

Jesus' Earthly Ministry Totally Under the Law

I'm embarrassed to admit how many years I've labored in ministry being ignorant of Paul's revelation in Rom. 15:8&9:

> Now I say that *Jesus Christ was a minister of the circumcision* [Jews] *for the truth of God, to confirm the promises made unto the fathers* [O.T. prophets, etc.]*; and that the Gentiles might glorify God for his mercy…* (emphasis mine).

Everything Jesus did was under the framework of the Law, for He came "not to destroy the Law, but to fulfill it." How pointed is Galatians 4:4,5 which says, "…When the fullness of the time was come, God sent forth His Son, made of a woman, *made under the law*, to redeem (deliver)them that were under the law…" He *filled full* the promises of the Old Testament "fathers" (prophets, etc.). Subsequently, Israel's rejection of the Perfect Messiah set up the crucifixion, by which the promised atonement for sin would be expedited (e.g. Isaiah 53, etc.) What a glorious mystery!

I've already stated that Pentecost was a Jewish holiday---Jews only! The believing disciples gathered "with one accord in one place," (2:1) when "suddenly" the Holy Spirit came. Were they expecting this manifestation or were they just meeting to celebrate the Feast? Were they "seeking the Holy Ghost" per se, or did He move unexpectedly (suddenly) in the midst of the Holy Day observance? Jesus did say, "tarry [wait] ye in the city…until ye be endued with power…" (Lk. 24:49). In Acts 1:8, Jesus simply states that they would "receive *power*" when the Spirit came, and they would be "witnesses unto me…" He did *not* say, "Ye shall receive *tongues*," although the varied languages mentioned served in the miraculous proclamation and spread of the Gospel.

Need we try to reenact this unique event? Do these facts warrant our "seeking Pentecost" in our day? Is the principle of the Holy

Spirit's "baptism of power" relative today? Absolutely! Just as the power of the Crucifixion is applicable by faith to a repentant sinner today; however, that doesn't require a historic reenactment of the once-for-all Cross-work of Jesus Christ. These are valid considerations if we're to properly understand this event.

Holy Spirit Evangelistic Campaign

It's significant that in Acts 2:5, it says that "there were dwelling at Jerusalem Jews, devout men out of every nation under heaven." It goes on to say that as the disciples spoke with "other tongues (languages);" the Jews who gathered for that occasion each "heard them speak in his own language." (vs. 6) This was a phenomenal and amazing manifestation of God's power! The following verses (9-11) list the countries from which these Jewish people came. Indeed, each person was now able to hear the message of the Messiah in his native tongue! No gibberish here, but the clear communication of the Gospel in known languages. Dr. H.D. Williams offers a vital observation here:

> The word "tongues" in English is translated from two different words. In v. 3 & 4, the Greek word is γλῶσσα (glossa); and in verse 8, "tongue" in the Greek is διάλεκτος (dialektos, which is translated "language" in verse 6). In other words, the Scripture does not infer that this was the language of "angels," or "ecstasy," or "heaven;" but rather the language [dialect] of people from the various nations attending the Day of Pentecost feast. Satan has cleverly led so many to falsely believe it is the language of the so-called "second baptism."

In reality and context, I would say that this was the first Holy Ghost Missionary Evangelistic Crusade, proclaiming the risen, glorified, and ascended Lord Jesus Christ! Amen!

This was in contrast to what happened at Babel in Gen. 11:1-9 where God brought confusion of language rather than clarity. The religious rebels who attempted to build a tower to reach God spoke "one language" which facilitated their wicked plan; the Lord in judgment stymied their work by confusing their speech, thwarting all communication. Significantly, the word "babel" means "confusion of voices." That was not the case at Pentecost where clear communication was evident as opposed to unintelligible "babbling." There was understanding and clarity to each person, regardless of their native language. Amazing!

What's the point here? In this Jewish Pentecostal feast setting, the Promised Holy Spirit is poured out on 120 believers as predicted by Jesus at a previous feast. In John 7:38-39, He says,

> He that believeth on me, as the scripture hath said, out of his belly shall flow rivers of living water. (But this spake he of the Spirit, which they that believe on him should receive; for the Holy Ghost was not yet *given*; because that Jesus was not yet glorified.)

This correlates with Jesus' promise to the disciples that He would give "another Comforter (Gr. *Paracletos*- intercessor, mediator) that he may abide with you forever; even the Spirit of truth...for he dwelleth with you, and *shall be in you*." (John 14:16-17; Italics mine)

This is the essence of Pentecost! Christ walked with them during His earthly ministry as "Emmanuel" meaning "God *with* us." (Matt.1:23) But now after His resurrection and ascension (Acts. 1) the Holy Spirit descends in mighty power to "invade" each believer, revealing the glorified Christ! No longer was it simply "God *with* us," but now God *in* us! As Jesus was "incarnated" in human flesh (John. 1:1, 14), so now was the

Holy Spirit "incarnated" into the believing assembly. (Revealed later as the Body of Christ) Now rather than Jesus just walking "with" them, He came to "live in" them forever! Thus, was the glorious implementation of Jesus promise, "I will never leave you, nor forsake you." How wonderful is that?

Oswald Chambers' Profound Observation:

I quote Oswald Chambers' keen insight regarding the glory of Pentecost:

> The disciples had to tarry, staying in Jerusalem until the day of Pentecost, not only for their own preparation but because they had to wait until the Lord was actually glorified. And as soon as He was glorified, what happened? "Therefore being exalted to the right hand of God, and having received from the Father the promise of the Holy Spirit, He poured out this which you now see and hear" (Acts 2:33). The statement in John 7:39— "…for the Holy Spirit was not yet given, because Jesus was not yet glorified"— does not pertain to us. The Holy Spirit has been given; the Lord is glorified— our waiting is not dependent on the providence of God, but on our own spiritual fitness.
>
> *The Holy Spirit's influence and power were at work before Pentecost, but He was not here. Once our Lord was glorified in His ascension, the Holy Spirit came into the world, and He has been here ever since.* We have to receive the revealed truth that He is here. *The attitude of receiving and welcoming the Holy Spirit into our lives is to be the continual attitude of a believer. When we receive the Holy Spirit, we receive reviving life from our ascended Lord.*
>
> *It is not the baptism of the Holy Spirit that changes people, but the power of the ascended Christ*

coming into their lives through the Holy Spirit. We all too often separate things that the New Testament never separates. *The baptism of the Holy Spirit is not an experience apart from Jesus Christ— it is the evidence of the ascended Christ.* (Italics mine) I say Amen!

CHAPTER 9

THE MYSTERY OF THE CHURCH (BODY OF CHRIST)

Biblical Events Timeline That We See Today Living in the Church Age

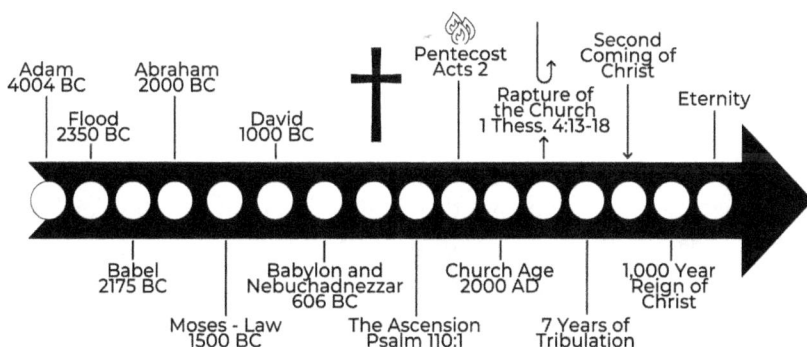

The Believer's Body—God's Sanctuary

Significantly, the Jewish temple in Jerusalem was destroyed in 70 AD by Rome, ending Israel's sacrificial system as practiced for 1500 years. The Passover Lamb (Jesus) was now offered, once-for-all; no more temporary "covering" of sin for a year (Atonement –Lev. 16), but complete forgiveness and removal of sin's curse! (cf. Heb. 1:3; 9:6-28; 10:19-22; John 1:29) Where's the temple then? The Apostle Paul makes it clear that in the Church Age the body of the believer in Christ becomes God's temple, indwelt by the Holy Spirit (cf. I Cor. 3:16; 6:19-20). Christ Jesus by His cross has made of two (Jew and Gentile) "one new man" (cf. Eph. 2:1-15). Both have been reconciled through Christ's redemptive work; so that neither a believing Jew or Gentile worship in a "temple" made with hands—they **are** the temple! God's Sanctuary, if you will. Hallelujah!

Believer and the Temple of God

Under the Old Covenant, the tabernacle (Ex.35f) was located in the midst of the 12 Tribes of Israel. Three tribes encamped in each side of that structure which "housed" the presence of Jehovah. He dwelt, as it were, in the midst of His people. Evidently, He wanted each tribe to have "access" to Him. Some 1500 years later, this same God "visits" earth in human form. John 1:14 says, "The Word became flesh and "dwelled [lit. tented, tabernacled] among us and we beheld His glory..." Jesus later said, "Where two or three are gathered together in my name, there as I in the midst," beautifully fulfilling the Old Testament type.

Yet because of Pentecost, this reality is taken to a higher level. Paul reveals that now the believer's body has become the tabernacle or temple of the Holy Spirit. (1 Cor. 6:19, 20) The Shekinah Glory resident in the O.T. temple has now been "transferred" to the saints who are now the "temple of God!" What was a stationary structure now becomes mobile again.
Furthermore, the terms Paul uses to describe this phenomenon are very significant. In 1 Corinthians 3:16, Paul reminds the saints that they are the "temple of God" (the inner sanctuary) in which dwells the Spirit of God. When using "temple" to designate the believer, he significantly uses the Greek word *naos*, which specifically depicts the dwelling place of God; i.e. the Holy of Holies or inner sanctuary. The only other word translated "temple" (e.g. Mk.11:11) is *heiron*, referring to the whole temple complex (i.e. outer courts, porches, chambers, etc.); therefore, since Pentecost, the child of God (Jew or Gentile) has become the "container" (dwelling place) of the Shekinah glory of Jehovah! That's almost unthinkable, but true! The same God who "resided" in Solomon's temple, now through Pentecost makes the believer in Messiah His abode on earth. Praise be to God!

76

Disciples' Pre-Pentecost Ignorance

For many years I pondered the significance of Jesus statement, "It is expedient for you that I go away; for if I go not away, the Comforter will not come unto you." (John 16:7) Obviously, the disciples would soon need "comfort" after Jesus left, but why was it necessary or "expedient" (lit. good, profitable) for Him to leave? Evidently, they needed the further equipping of Pentecost in order to effectively spread the Kingdom Gospel worldwide (Acts 1:8). Time and again, Jesus rebukes their ignorance and unbelief. They "walked" with Him, but did they really know who He was? When Jesus questioned the 12 as to His true identity, they were stumped. Finally, Peter confesses that He (Jesus) "was the Christ, the son of the living God..." (Matt.16:16). But this was "revealed" to Peter by the Father; it was otherwise unknown, especially to the other 11 men. This probably explains why Peter lingered at the Cross scene, while the other disciples ran away. If Jesus was the reigning Messiah, how could He be taken and killed? I think that this seeming "contradiction" triggered unbelief in Peter's heart, resulting in his temporary denial.

This illustrates their necessity to be "indwelt and filled" with the Holy Spirit in order to really know Christ intimately. May I carefully say that a Spirit-filled believer today may know more about Jesus personally than the disciples did *prior* to Pentecost? There's a difference between the "upon-dwelling" and the "indwelling" of the Holy Spirit. Likewise, as intimated earlier, there is a valid distinction between the "filling" and the "fullness" of the Spirit.

It is significant that the disciples were so ignorant of many things Jesus taught. How often did Jesus exhort them regarding His crucifixion, for instance, and they never got it. One such example is Luke 18:31f, where He clearly foretells his being delivered to the "Gentiles...who shall scourge him, and put him to death; and the third day he shall rise again." But the writer goes on to say that "they [the disciples] understood none of these things." How could that be? Because "this saying was hid from them, neither knew they the things which were spoken." For His own reason, God saw fit to withhold from them the fact of the coming Crucifixion of their Messiah.

Power of the Empty Tomb

Even the faithful ladies, who approached the empty tomb following the Resurrection, were "perplexed" and "afraid" when asked by the two angels, "Why seek ye the living among the dead?" But they soon "remembered his (Jesus) words" (cf. Lk. 24:5-8); however, when these eye-witnesses returned to the "eleven" to relate their experience, Luke says that "their words seemed to them [disciples] as idle tales, and they believed them not." (Lk. 24:11) Wow! With that Peter runs to the sepulcher to see for himself. John's account relates how he and Peter, when seeing the grave clothes and napkin, they "saw and *believed*, for as yet they knew not the scripture, that he must rise again from the dead." (cf. John 20:1-9) This seems to be the turning point of Peter's doubt and delusion. He was an "unbelieving believer" up to this time, for he could not fathom how the revealed Messiah could ever be anything but the reigning Millennial King!

To those of you in leadership ministry there's a practical and helpful lesson gleaned from the above scenario. How did Jesus "put up" with the obvious unbelief and ignorance of the disciples? I believe He chose to see them not for what they were at that present time, but for what they would be after the "baptism (invasion) of the Spirit" at Pentecost. This principle has greatly helped me to be patient in working with immature and difficult believers; yes, they're not what they should be, but we must anticipate their growth in grace as they learn to appropriate the Spirit's fullness. Considering this critical time in church history, Paul's admonition to Timothy is most appropriate for any pastor:

> Preach the word; be instant in season, out of season; reprove, rebuke, exhort with all longsuffering and doctrine. For the time will come when they will not endure sound doctrine; but after their own lusts shall they heap to themselves teachers, having itching ears; And they shall turn away their ears from the truth, and shall be turned unto fables. But watch thou in all things, endure afflictions, do the work of an evangelist, make full proof of thy ministry (2 Tim. 4:2-5).

I would be remiss if I didn't make mention of Jesus' post-resurrection appearance to the disciples in the upper room. (cf. John 20:19f) They (disciples) were gathered in fear of the Jews and Jesus stood in the midst to comfort their hearts. He says, "Peace be unto you; as my Father hath send me, even so send I you. And when he had said this, he breathed *on* them, and saith...Receive ye the Holy Ghost." (John 20: 21&22) What was this about? In context, it had to be a distinct gesture of confirmation and encouragement bestowed upon this fearful, still "perplexed" rag-tag group. It was a foretaste of the Coming Spirit's baptism that would fully equip and enable them to fulfill Christ's commission. This was still a pre-Pentecost event, but we could say that it was a "preview of coming attractions."

The Spirit Dispels Ignorance

Evidently, Isaiah 53's depiction of the Suffering Savior was obscured from Peter's mind. What appeared to be Peter's "rejection or denial" of Christ, was really his profound uncertainty as to Jesus' true identity. This doubt was certainly removed at the empty tomb. Moreover, it was just a matter of days before Peter would experience the mighty invasion of the

Holy Spirit's fullness (indwelling and upon-dwelling), empowering him to be God's spokesman at Pentecost. (cf. Acts 2:14f) His faith and mission were now bolstered and confirmed by this event. I believe that this was the initiation of a new phase or level of Jesus' personal ministry now from Heaven by His Spirit—the Third Person of the Trinity. This was the fulfillment of Jesus' promise regarding His coming ascension to Heaven:

> If ye love me, keep my commandments. And I will pray *the Father*, and he *shall give you another Comforter, that he may abide with you forever. Even the Spirit of truth*; whom the world cannot receive, because it seeth him not, neither knoweth him; but ye know him; *for he dwelleth with you, and shall be in you.* I will not leave you comfortless [lit. orphans]: *I will come to you.* (John 14:15-18; italics mine)

Notice the interaction of the divine Trinity in the above passage. Jesus says, "I will pray the Father, and he [the Father] will give you another Comforter *(allon parakleton)*..." The Gr. *allon* means "another of the same kind;" not *heteron*, used of a "different kind." One just like Jesus, the third Person of the Godhead, would come as their Comforter or Mediator; only now He would actually live within them! Wow! How else could they have intimate fellowship with the now-Glorified Jesus Christ whom they could not see or touch?

Further, He says, "I will come to you;" Jesus never came back in flesh, but rather at Pentecost He comes as the Spirit of Christ, making believers His dwelling place (Sanctuary)! (cf. Col. 1:27, 1Cor. 3:16) Jesus now becomes the believer's Paraclete, meaning Comforter, Helper, Mediator, and Advocate, with the Father (1John 2:1; cf. Rom. 8:26) RWP delivers a profound statement, "So the Christian has Christ as his Paraclete with the

Father, (and) the Holy Spirit as the Father's Paraclete with us (John 14:16, 26; 15:26; 16:7)" For how long? **Forever!** How mysteriously wonderful is that? Hallelujah!

The Spirit's Regenerating Work in the Old Testament

It's important to understand the unique significance of this "coming" of the Holy Spirit. His ministry is prolific throughout the Old Testament, empowering the servants of Jehovah for various tasks, etc. The prophets speak of the Spirit "coming upon them" or even entering "in them" (cf. Ezek. 2:2); but it always seems to depict a temporary event. Obviously, the Old Testament believers were saved through the regenerating work of the Holy Spirit by faith in God's blood sacrifice. We must emphasize that saving grace throughout Biblical history has always involved the shedding of innocent blood and faith in that provision. (cf. Heb. 11:6)

Abraham, for instance, "believed God and it was counted unto him as righteousness;" he took God at His word, along with offering blood sacrifice. (cf. Genesis 15) Under the Mosaic Law, the annual Passover and Day of Atonement involved shedding the blood of innocent animals to atone or "cover" the sins of the people for a year. But this was temporary and ongoing, anticipating the future, complete redemptive work of Jehovah's Servant (cf. Isa. 53; John 1:29).

Yes, even King David was saved by grace, but not without offering a blood sacrifice. Like others, he had to come with a lamb or goat to the temple to "compliment" his faith in God's ordained provision of salvation and forgiveness. That innocent animal was offered up to atone for man's guilt and sin. This system carried through the entire Old Testament and into the New. The Gospels are really an ongoing extension or progression of the Old Covenant; as previously mentioned, Jesus was incarnated into a totally legal setting; everything He did was under the Mosaic system, for He said, "I came not to destroy the law, but to fulfill it." Even as a child, He was brought by His parents to Jerusalem "to present him to the Lord...according to that which is said in the Law of the Lord..." (cf. Lk. 2:22-27)

We must reiterate that "the law was given to Moses, but grace and truth came by Jesus Christ;" yet, Christ's earthly ministry was primarily to Israel, with some exception.(e.g. Syrophoenician woman – Mk.7:24f) This thought was confirmed when I was eventually confronted with Matthew 10:5ff, where Jesus sent forth the twelve and commanded them, saying,

> **Go not** into the way of the Gentiles, and into any city of the Samaritans [half-Jews] enter ye *not*; *but go rather to the lost sheep of* the house of *Israel*. And...preach, saying, the kingdom of heaven is at hand. (vs.5-7; emphasis mine)

This was the "Kingdom Gospel" for Israel, whose Messiah had come to reign. They (the twelve) were also commissioned to "heal the sick, cleanse the lepers, and raise the dead..." These signs and miracles were to authenticate the LORD's coming, especially since the "Jews required a sign." Without these the LORD would not have gotten their attention.

What actually happened at Pentecost is much more profound and mysterious than the present-day emphasis on the "miraculous" and experiential. In fact, I would say, as others, that the event of Pentecost has been greatly underestimated. What did Jesus imply when He said, "It is *expedient* that I go away or the Comforter will not come?" The answer really defies human understanding, for it involves the mysterious inter-action of the Godhead (Trinity). Jesus is referring to His Ascension to Heaven, as well as His "incarnation" or invasion into the waiting disciples on earth.

CHAPTER 10

SIGNIFICANCE OF CHRIST'S ASCENSION

It was vitally important that Jesus left (ascended from) this world after the Crucifixion and before Pentecost. It was imperative that His redemptive work be accomplished *prior* to the "dispensing" or coming of the Holy Spirit. The "invasion" (indwelling) of the Spirit of necessity must *follow* the completed sacrificial work of Christ. John states, "When Jesus therefore received the vinegar, he said, **It is finished**; and he bowed his head and gave up the ghost." (John 20:30) What was "finished?' All that was necessary to save a world of sinners (past, present, and future) was accomplished by the Lord Jesus Christ at the Cross! Every Old Testament feast, offering, prophecy, type, and shadow was totally fulfilled in and by Jesus Christ!

As the prophet said, "All we like sheep have gone astray; we have turned every one to his own way; and the LORD hath laid on Him the iniquity of us all." (Isa. 53:6) Not only that, but He was "set forth to be a propitiation through faith in his blood..." (Rom. 3:25); i.e. He took the full wrath of God in our place; He fully satisfied the justice of Jehovah that was breached (violated) by sinful man. God looked at His suffering servant at Calvary and said, "My holiness is satisfied (propitiated, appeased) in the perfect sacrifice of my Son" (cf. Isa. 53: 10, 11). Amen!

Hear Matthew Henry's comment

Matthew Henry's comment is worth noting:

> *It is finished*, that is, the ceremonial law is abolished, and a period put to the obligation of it.

The substance is now come, and all the shadows are done away. Just now *the veil is rent, the wall of partition is taken down, even the law of commandments contained in ordinances*, Eph. 2:14, 15.

The work of man's redemption and salvation is now completed..; a full satisfaction is made to the justice of God, a fatal blow given the power of Satan, a fountain of grace opened that shall ever flow, a foundation of peace and happiness laid that shall never fail. Christ had now gone through with his work, and *finished it*, Joh 17:4. For, *as for God, his work is perfect*; *when I begin*, saith he, *I will also make an end.* (italics mine)

Sin Removed

We must never overlook the glorious fulfillment of John 1:29, where the Baptist cried, "Behold, the Lamb of God, which *taketh away the sin of the world.*" The Old Testament sacrifices were ordained of God to deal with Israel's sin by the shedding of innocent animal blood; but none of these sacrifices or offerings was permanent or complete. The Passover lamb was sacrificed each year, and the blood was applied by faith to each Israelite's doorway; when sin's judgment was to be poured out by the death angel, God said, "When I see the blood, I will pass over you;" i.e. none will die in that household (Ex.12). This was temporary, even though Passover is still celebrated by Judaism to this day (*without* a slain lamb!). But through God's eternal Lamb, sin has been taken away permanently!

Likewise, the Day of Atonement (Yom Kippur) was the annual high and holy day when Israel's sin would be "atoned for" (Heb. *Kaphar*, meaning "to cover, appease, or forgive"). Leviticus 16:1-34 describes the specific details of this most

84

solemn feast Day of Israel. (The reader is encouraged to prayerfully study this passage for its tremendous insight, as well as the unique layout of the Tabernacle proper; cf. Ex. 25-40)

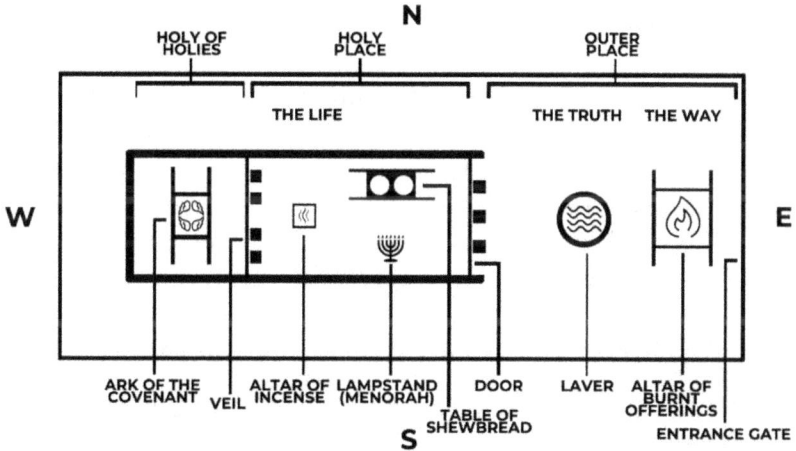

Simply stated, Moses received the Moral Law (Ten Commandments – Ex. 20), which Israel broke. Thankfully, God, anticipating their failure, gave Moses the Ceremonial Law intricately connected to the Tabernacle. Here the Lord would establish a sacrificial system whereby He could temporarily deal with or forgive their sin **(See above diagram)**. Entering the only door (East), into the outer court, the priests ministered before the Lord via the brazen altar and the laver; there was a curtain which opened into the Holy Place, containing the table of showbread, the lampstand (menorah) and altar of incense; then approaching the third or inner-most area was the veil which separated the Holy Place from the Holy of Holies (Holiest of All). It was here that the Ark of the Covenant was housed. Covering the Ark was the Mercy Seat (golden slab), upon which the atoning blood was sprinkled on this occasion; herein was the presence of God (Shekinah Glory) manifested. No one could enter into this area except Aaron, the High Priest, and not without the sacrificial blood, and only once a year. Any "mistake" here resulted in his sudden death!

On this Holy Day, the high priest had to first offer a bull as a sin offering for himself and his family. The blood of the bull was then sprinkled upon the Ark of the Covenant. Then Aaron brought two goats, one to be sacrificed for Israel's sin and rebellion. That goat's blood was also sprinkled on the Ark (Mercy Seat). The second goat was used as a "scapegoat," but equally part of the sacrifice for atonement. Aaron placed his hands on its head, confessed over it the sin of the Israelites, and sent that goat into the wilderness. This innocent animal "carried away" the sins of the people, who were forgiven for another year. The word for "scapegoat" (vs.10) is *azazel*, meaning "goat of departure or removal."

Christ's Full and Eternal Atonement

What's the significance of all this to the New Covenant? The two goats beautifully portray (typify) the sufficiency and completeness of Christ's sacrifice. The first goat's blood sprinkled on the Ark typified the appeasement of God's wrath (i.e. Propitiation; Rom. 3:25; 5:9); the second goat removed the sins of the people into the wilderness to be forgotten; this is called Expiation, the act of atoning for sin and removing it from the sinner. The Psalmist says, "as far as the east is from the west, so far hath He *removed* our transgressions from us." (Psa. 103:12) Heb. 10:17 adds, "And their sins and iniquities will I *remember no more.*"

How marvelous was that provision for sins; but it "covered" them just for one year, and then had to be repeated. Both of these aspects for sin, however, were achieved *eternally* by Christ's sacrifice of Himself on the Cross! Listen to excerpts from Hebrews and worship! (emphasis mine)

> **But Christ being come an high priest of good things to come, by a greater and more perfect tabernacle, not made with hands, that is to say, not of this building; Neither by the blood**

of goats and calves, but by his own blood he entered in once into the holy place, having obtained eternal redemption *for us*... (Heb. 9:11-12)

For Christ is not entered into the holy places made with hands, which are the figures of the true; but into heaven itself, now to appear in the presence of God for us: Nor yet that he should offer himself often, as the high priest entereth into the holy place every year with blood of others; For then must he often have suffered since the foundation of the world: **but now once** in the end of the world **hath he appeared to put away sin** by the sacrifice of himself. And **as it is appointed unto men once to die, but after this the judgment: So Christ was once offered to bear the sins of many;** and unto them that look for him shall he appear the second time without sin unto salvation. (Heb. 9:24-28; cf. 10:9-14)

CHAPTER 11

LIVING ON THE RIGHT SIDE OF THE CROSS

Why am I laboring this point of the *finished*, "once-for-all" atoning work of Christ? Because, among other things, this was the heart of the message of Pentecost; i.e. the Old Covenant was fulfilled in Christ and the New ushered in. The Ascension was Christ's unique and perfect presentation of His full Redemption before the Father in Heaven. This *package* of Christ's complete work of Salvation was now ready to be *delivered* in totality at Pentecost. Not to diminish in anyway the outpouring of the Spirit's power, but there was much more involved in this divine infusion. By the Holy Spirit, this was not just an "incarnation" of the *earthly* Jesus into the waiting believers, but a personal and permanent invasion of the *Glorified* Messiah! For the first time, Christ's finished work was to permeate every fiber of the believer's being by the indwelling Spirit! (cf. Eph. 1:15f; 3:10f; 5:18)

Mary Magdalene's Unique Confrontation

John records a unique event of Mary Magdalene's meeting in the garden with her risen Savior. (John 0:11-18) There's an obvious mystique which surrounds this event, which has challenged the best of commentators. Having sadly peered into the empty tomb, she turns and notices Jesus, whom she thinks is the gardener. He (Jesus) reveals his identity by calling her name, "Mary;" but something is radically different than before; then He makes a most baffling statement: "Touch me not; for I am not yet ascended to my Father; but go to my brethren, and say unto them, I ascend unto my Father, *and to your Father*; and to my God, *and your God*." (John 20:17; italics mine)

It's almost like Heaven and earth come together here; Mary is in Jesus presence but something is different; she may have reached out to "touch" Him as before the Cross, but Jesus retorts, "Touch me not." I'm sure that Mary could have been rebuffed by this response when compared to her prior earthly relationship with Jesus; but now in His resurrected state, Jesus is ready to ascend into Heaven to present the culmination of His finished earthly work before the Father. No human "touch" or contact could be allowed to taint the unique sanctity of such an awesome and eternal transaction.

Significantly, Jesus makes a clear distinction between His deity and humanity. He says, "I ascend unto *my Father," and your Father; and to my God, and your God.*" Jesus has a unique and eternal relationship with His Father (John 1:1f), not shared with or by any earthly being. He used the term "Our Father" in the so-called "Lord's Prayer" when teaching the disciples to pray (Matt. 6:9f); but I submit that He was not including Himself in that prayer. This instructive prayer was to be used by His followers (even today). The valid and personal "Lord's Prayer" with His Father is found in the 17th Chapter of John's Gospel. While He identified with humanity, His deity and relationship with His Father were totally unique. (cf. Phil. 2:5-11) Paul states in 1Tim. 2:5, "… there is one God, and one mediator between God and man, the man Christ Jesus." This was possible since Jesus Christ was the God-Man, i.e. He was indeed fully man and fully God! How awesome and mystifying is this thought? As a fellow-servant often says, "There's no one like Jesus, **No One!**"

Heavenly Invasion of Christ into Believers

I use the above episode with Mary to further demonstrate the "expediency" of Jesus' glorious ascension and the wondrous aftermath. All the fulfillment of Old Testament types, offerings, shadows, etc. crescendos into this marvelous event, and ushers in a whole new dimension of God's progressive program. By this outpouring (descent) of the Holy Spirit at Pentecost, the ascended Christ "invaded" the bodies of His disciples! This truth has to be one of the most sublime and mind-boggling teachings in the entire Bible. Paul addresses the reality of the "indwelling Christ" in various places; e.g. Gal. 1:15, 16; 2:20; Eph. 3:16, 17; Rom. 8:9, 10. Let us consider briefly his teaching on the matter recorded in Colossians. 1:25-27:

> Whereof I am made a minister, according to the dispensation of God which is given to me for you, to fulfil the word of God; Even the mystery which hath been hid from ages and from generations, but now is made manifest to his saints: To whom God would make known what is the riches of the glory of this mystery among the Gentiles; which is *Christ in you, the hope of glory.* (italics mine)

It is essential that we never lose sight of the Apostle Paul's unique ministry in revealing the divine "mystery" of the church or body of Christ which had been "hidden" throughout the past ages. Israel never heard of the body of Christ (church), nor is it mentioned in the Gospels. In His sovereignty, the Lord saw fit to hide that truth until after the "dispensing" of the Holy Spirit at Pentecost; Paul now "opens" or reveals this glorious "mystery" of the indwelling Christ; but, wonder of wonders, this Gift is provided not only for the Jew, but the despised "Gentile dogs" as well! (cf. Matt. 15:21-28; Eph. 2:11-13) Here God makes known (accessible) "the riches of the glory of this *mystery among the Gentiles*;" What mystery was that? "**Christ in you**, the hope of glory!" That is to say, there is absolutely no hope of eternal salvation (Glory) for any sinner (Jew or Gentile) apart from the saving, indwelling Christ!

Adam Clarke comments: "He (Paul) proclaimed this Christ as being in them; for the design of the Gospel is to put men in possession of the Spirit and power of Christ, to make them

91

partakers of the Divine nature, and thus prepare them for an eternal union with himself." Amen.

Daniel Whittle captures this thought in his song "Christ Liveth in Me:"

> Once far from God and dead in sin; no light my heart could see; but in God's Word the light I found, Now Christ liveth in me; As lives the flow'r within the seed, As in the cone the tree; So, praise the God of truth and grace, His Spirit dwelleth in me; With longing all my heart is filled, That like Him I may be; As on the wondrous tho't I dwell, That Christ liveth in me. Chorus: Christ liveth in me, Christ liveth in me; Oh! What a salvation this, That Christ liveth in me!

Seeing that the Holy Spirit's ministry is to "glorify" and reveal Christ, the focus is now on the ascended, heavenly Jesus Christ; this means that the "unseen" Savior is presently living out His resurrection life in and through His Spirit-filled children! Wow!

Since Pentecost, there's been a unique intimacy with the Holy Spirit whereby the very character of Christ is "worked in and out" through the believer. (cf. Phil. 2:12, 13) This phenomenon is called the "fruit of the Spirit" described in Galatians 5:22 &23; i.e. "love, joy, peace, longsuffering, gentleness, goodness, faith, meekness, temperance [self-control]; against such there is no law." Unlike the "works" of the Law, this 9-fold fruit is "planted" in the believer's heart by virtue of the indwelling Spirit of God; thus, the very life of Christ is evidenced and fulfilled in and through the Christian. This accounts for the ongoing ministry of Christ on earth through His Body (the Church).

No wonder He said, "Greater things will ye do because I go to my Father..." After all, Jesus of Nazareth probably never travelled more than one hundred miles from home. How incredibly that was changed, not only in geographic outreach, but in the Heavenly authority and resurrection nature of the Message. A.J. Gordon explains here that "Jesus returned to a Glorified state (different than earthly ministry—another level of glory)." This is the One who now resides within the believer because of Pentecost.

CHAPTER 12
THE ECONOMY OF GRACE

When Paul speaks of "the dispensation of the grace of God" (Eph. 3:2), he's not suggesting that we now "discard" the Old Testament or "cut up" the Bible into several epochs of time. The word "dispensation" has become a point of contention because of misunderstanding and/or theological bias. "Dispensation" (Gr. *oikonomia*) stems from the verb "to manage, administer, or regulate." The common usage was that of a manager or steward who administered the affairs of a household. (cf. Lk. 12:42; 16:1f; 1 Cor. 4:1, 2) According to Vincent, Paul uses the term to express "divine government or regulation of the world."

Someone has concisely defined a dispensation as a "distinguishable economy in the outworking of God's purpose." The distinguishing (distinctive) features are introduced by God; the similar features are retained by God; and the overall combined purpose of the whole program is the glory of God. W. Graham Scroggie, a noted Scottish writer and pastor, gave this helpful definition:

> The word oikonomia bears one significance, and means "an administration," whether of a house, or property, of a state, or a nation, or as in the present study, the administration of the human race or any part of it, at any given time. Just as a parent would govern his household in different ways, according to varying necessity, yet ever for one good end, so God has at different times dealt with men in different ways, according to the necessity of the case, but throughout for one great, grand end.

Progressive Dispensationalism

Personally, I lean heavily toward what is known as "progressive dispensationalism;" that dispensations are not just different arrangements between God and man; but *successive arrangements* in the progressive revelation and achievement of man's redemption. We see this sovereign progression of revelation throughout Scripture. The God who gave Abraham the covenant blessing of his seed in Genesis 12 is the same God who dispensed the Law to Moses (Ex.19f). The plan or economy of God continued to progress until John the Baptist introduced the Messiah who was to reign over the earth. Israel's rejection of the Christ did not stop God's ongoing plan, but led into the "dispensation (dispensing) of Grace." It's the same God, but a different economy.

Significantly, Jesus' first mention of His departure from the disciples is recorded in Mark. 2:20 in the context of fasting. In the following two verses, He (Jesus) speaks of the futility of patching an old torn garment with a new piece of cloth, resulting in a larger tear; likewise He mentions the mismatch of placing new wine in an old wine skin (bottle), eventually by fermentation, bursting the bottle. I believe this simply illustrates the progressive distinction of the Old and New Covenants; between the Old sacrificial or ceremonial law, and the final Cross-work of Messiah. Again, this verifies the theme of Hebrews that the Old Covenant was "good," but the New is "better!"

For many years I tried to force Paul's Gospel (1 Cor. 15:1-4) into the whole of Scripture; I couldn't bear the thought that there might be any "disruption" or inconsistency in God's plan of Salvation. Then I was faced with Abraham's salvation experience in Genesis 15 where it says that he "believed in the LORD; and He (God) counted it to him for righteousness." He believed "what"? Was it the Gospel of Christ's death, burial, and resurrection per se? Obviously not; he simply took God at His word by faith, along with a sacrificial offering, and God's righteousness was imputed to him.

Abraham and Grace

Paul, in Romans 4, cites this example of justifying grace through faith apart from any works done by Abraham. He says, "if Abraham were justified by works, he hath whereof to glory [boast], but not before God...But him that *worketh not, but believeth* on him that justifieth the ungodly, *his faith is counted for righteousness.*" (emphasis mine) You say, "Wait a minute, didn't Abraham have to keep the Law (Ten Commandments)?" That was not a factor here seeing that the Law of Moses did not arrive until some 430 years *after* Abraham; however, the "law of faith" has been operating throughout all of Biblical history. This demonstrates that at any given time, saving grace was "dispensed" to those who believed God and honored the blood sacrifice (i.e. the offering of innocent life for the guilty).

John's message of "repent and be baptized for the remission of sins..." was transitional, announcing the Kingdom of God to Israel. (cf. Matt. 3:1, 2; Mk. 1:4; Acts.2:38) This Gospel included not only repentant faith, but ceremonial washing (baptism) stemming from O.T ordinances. Like Moses or Solomon before them, their faith in God had to be accompanied by an animal blood sacrifice. So here in the Gospels, Israel was still under the Law, as was Jesus. Remember, that "Jesus Christ was a minister of the circumcision [Jews] for the truth of God, to confirm the promises made unto the fathers" (Rom. 15:8). Jesus fulfilled all righteousness under the Law (in His life and death) so that "justification by faith in Christ *alone* might be "dispensed."

I hate to think of how long I attempted to fit the "Kingdom Gospel" of Acts. 2:38 into the message of Grace. I couldn't square this with Galatians 2:16 which emphatically says,

"Knowing that a man is not justified by the works of the law, but by the faith of Jesus Christ..." When the Philippian jailer asked, "What must I do to be saved?" Paul replied, "Believe on the Lord Jesus Christ and thou shalt be saved..." (Acts 16:31) To the Romans, Paul exhorted,

> That if thou shalt confess with thy mouth the Lord Jesus, and shalt believe in thine heart that God hath raised him from the dead, thou shalt be saved. For with the heart man believeth unto righteousness; and with the mouth confession is made unto salvation. (Rom. 10:9&10)

Does that mean that John the Baptist's or Peter's "Kingdom" message was wrong? Certainly not! It was God's ordained "Gospel" to His people Israel, introducing Messiah. They were saved by "believing on His Name;" i.e. The Messiah (e.g. Acts 4:12: John20:31) The Gospel of Grace, however, was later revealed to the Apostle Paul (cf. Gal. 1, 2); he clearly states and defines this saving Gospel in 1 Cor. 15:1-4:

> Moreover, brethren, I declare unto you *the gospel* which I preached unto you, which also ye have received, and wherein ye stand; *By which also ye are saved*, if ye keep in memory what I preached unto you, unless ye have believed in vain. For I delivered unto you first of all that which I also received, how that *Christ died for our sins* according to the scriptures; And that *he was buried, and that he rose again* the third day according to the scriptures. (italics mine)

The Apostle of Grace

While some believed, Israel's overall rejection of the Christ was met by God's saving call in Acts 9 to a fanatical Jew named Saul (Paul). The Lord commissions him as "a chosen vessel unto me, to bear my name before the Gentiles, and kings, and the children of Israel." (Acts. 9:15). This advanced scenario is beautifully described by Paul himself in his message to "the men of Israel" in Acts 13:16ff. (*A must read*)

It's significant that no one preached the "death, burial, and resurrection of Christ" prior to Pentecost; first, it hadn't happened yet; and second, this became the theme of Paul's Gospel of Grace (1 Cor. 15:3&4). This was a new "economy" of God's progressive plan to reach the world of Gentiles, along with individual Jews. This accounts for the Church's extending westward into the world. Many of us would still be lost in sin if the Temple worship were essential to salvation. After all, the Temple in Jerusalem was destroyed by Rome in 70 AD. As we have discussed, it was God's ordained message to Israel that the day of animal sacrifice, etc. was over! Now Christ's finished work at Calvary was all-sufficient for Salvation. This was all part of the ongoing work (economy, dispensing) of the Holy Spirit.

CHAPTER 13

THE UNIQUE WORK OF THE HOLY SPIRIT IN ACTS

Notice how the Third Person of the Godhead is prominent in Acts. For example, the Holy Spirit not only "baptized" 120 into the Body of Christ (Act. 2:4f), but later "filled" various leaders of the church (assembly); e.g. Peter (4:8); first deacons (6:3-5); Stephen (7:55); Barnabas (11:22, 24); and Paul (13:8).

Moreover, it's significant to observe how the Holy Spirit also gave oversight to the early Church ministry:

1. He appointed officers – 20:17, 28
2. He sent out missionaries – 13:2, 4
3. He directed missionaries – 8:29, 39 (Philip); 16:6-9 (Paul)
4. He comforted (encouraged) churches – 9:31
5. His ultimate authority and approval of the "dispensation of the Gospel of grace" (Eph. 3:2) was finally confirmed by the Jerusalem Council with that classic phrase: "...it seemed good to the Holy Ghost, and to us..." – 15:28

It should also be noted that in chapter five, where Peter confronts Ananias' hypocrisy, he says, "...why hath Satan filled thine heart to lie to the *Holy Ghost...*?" (vs.3) Soon after, his wife Sapphira appeared on the scene and was likewise confronted with her part in the "scheme." Peter says, "How is it that ye have agreed together to tempt the *Spirit of the Lord?*" Again, the person of the Holy Spirit, the Third member of the Godhead, is addressed, rather than the Father or the Son. Until more recently, I have never given that much thought; but, along with afore-mentioned facts, it appears that Acts introduces a "new" or progressive economy (dispensation) of the Holy Spirit's work.

The Father's ministry certainly engulfs the Old Testament revelation, while Jesus the Son is the Focus of the Gospels during His earthly ministry. I would thus submit that *Pentecost further propels the continuing ministry (program) of the Father and the Son through the ongoing work of the Holy Spirit.* Therefore, there's no need to "go back" to Pentecost for anything; the same is true regarding those of us who would like to "recapture" the glory of the Reformation," the "Puritan Era," or some mighty revival, etc. It all sounds so right and desirable, but it's all wishful thinking; that's all history! That was "then," but this is "now!"

I know this is a hard "pill" for some of us to swallow, but let's face it, there's no way to relive the past; but what about the future? What about the Spirit-filled 144,000 Jewish evangelists who will preach the Gospel to the ends of the earth during the seven year Tribulation period? (cf. Rev. 7, 14). An innumerable multitude will come to the Lamb of God, making this the greatest revival the world has ever seen; not to mention, the "greater than Pentecost" when Messiah returns to earth at the close of the Tribulation; at that time, "the Spirit of grace" will be poured out on Israel, and they will bow at His feet in repentant faith. (cf. Zech.12:9-12) This is the same Spirit who is operating today. God is "up to something" **now**, and thankfully, His undiminished fullness is still available! It's too soon to quit!

Present-Day Application of the Spirit's Power

I want to be careful not to discourage saints from praying for widespread, national awakening. If the Church should "come alive" and be revived in the Spirit, who knows what God would do in our beloved country? Our God is Sovereign and can do whatever He chooses, to whatever extent. In the meantime, the issue is what does the Lord desire to accomplish in my present life and ministry? Hopefully, we have established the fact that whatever I need now to serve God is totally accessible, without trying to reenact the day of Pentecost. (Phil. 4:13)

I've been made aware that there are present-day movements (e.g. the New Apostolic Reformation, "New Calvinism," etc.) which are attempting to literally "continue" the apostolic ministry surrounding Pentecost. They have taken the "Word of Faith" or "Prosperity Gospel" to another level. They are "ordaining" young men and women as prophets and apostles to duplicate or "pick up" where the church in Acts left off. In other words, they are attempting to "return" to Pentecost, and the original "apostleship," endeavoring to bring the Spirit's power "up to date." This seems to be an effort to invade and subdue the world, thereby bringing in God's Kingdom to earth. That may be a lofty motive, but the LORD alone, not the church, will one day establish His Kingdom on earth (cf. Dan. 7:13f; Rev. 19:11ff); however, until He comes, it still pleases God "by the foolishness of preaching to save them who believe," one sinner at a time.(1 Cor.1:21)

John Wesley's Experience

The story is told of John Wesley, the 18th C. British missionary to America. As I understand it, he was sailing across the Atlantic when he met a Moravian missionary; who asked him (Wesley) if he had ever been "filled with the Spirit?" John was disturbed, especially when the missionary further exhorted him not to preach to anyone without God's power. John arrived at his new home with this challenge on his heart. He wrestled daily for days, pleading for the Spirit's fullness. He prayed for hours on Monday, but sensed nothing of the Spirit. He continued in his prayerful pursuit throughout that week, but to no avail. At the end of the week, as he prayed, the verse "Go ye into all the world and preach the Gospel to every creature…" captured his mind. With that, he decided to get up and start down the road to "seek souls." He soon met a man at the end of the path who asked if he were Mr. Wesley. As John responded, the man began to share that he was a needy soul, seeking salvation and hoping John could help him. Wesley related later that during that "divine appointment" the "Holy Spirit filled him!" Obedience and "filling" are somehow related. Amen!

Pentecost Includes All True Believers

Not to labor the point, but after all these years of ministry I see the reality of Pentecost as more than just an "outpouring" of the Holy Spirit. A whole new and progressive era of Church history was inaugurated. The book of Acts was more than just transitional from the Gospels; it opened the door to *world* evangelization. Acts 1-8 focus on the area of Jerusalem, but Paul's conversion (Acts 9) begins the outreach to Gentiles, which was despised by Judaism. The missionary journeys of Paul extended church plants to the "uttermost parts" of the then-known world. The Holy Spirit further inspired the apostle's letters (some 14) to govern and instruct those churches.

We could say that the Holy Spirit took the "external" work of Christ on earth and applied it "internally" within the believer. Christ was the visible manifestation of the invisible God-Head (cf. John 14:6; Col. 1:14, 15; Heb. 1:3); so the Christian makes Christ "visible" in the world through the "invisible" Spirit of Christ living within. (1Cor. 6:19&20)

This was that "expedient" factor in preparation for the Comforter's descent at Pentecost. When the Holy Spirit entered ("baptized") the waiting believers, this complete sacrifice of Calvary was included and revealed. The full brunt of Eternal Salvation gripped them! Notice also that *all* 120 received the "baptism!" No one was left out; i.e. there were no "haves" and "have nots." In fact, in all the other "mini-Pentecosts" throughout Acts, the Spirit baptized only *groups* of believers, *not* individuals per se. (cf. Acts 8 – Samaritans; Acts 10 – God-fearers, e.g. Cornelius; Acts 19 – Gentiles)

I've been amazed by the many disagreements existing on that latter subject; and how the understanding of future revelation hinges directly on a proper understanding of Pentecost. I'm convinced that while God is not giving new revelation, as some of these heretical groups profess, He *is* granting fresh illumination on Bible revelation as the Day approaches.

CHAPTER 14

WHAT IS THE EVIDENCE OF THE SPIRIT'S FULLNESS?

Gifts Versus Fruit

I think it significant that Jesus said, "By their *fruit* ye shall know them..." (cf. Gal. 5:22-23) The "gifts" come out of the fruit, not the other way around. The "love" (fruit) chapter (1 Cor. 13) is "sandwiched" between the "gifts" chapters (12 & 14); not to nullify the gifts, but to emphasize the ineffectiveness of the gifts without the Spirit's fruit. It's been said, for instance, that one who simply professes to "speak in "tongues" proves only one thing; that he "speaks in tongues!" The "gifts" of the Spirit without the "fruit" of the Spirit are futile and powerless; Paul says, "Though I speak with the tongues of men and of angels, and have not charity [love], I am become as sounding brass, or a tinkling cymbal..." (cf. 1 Cor. 13:1-3) That "dull and tinny" sound is not only useless, but detrimental to the cause of Christ. The airwaves and churches are replete with charlatans and false teachers who use their "fruitless gifts" to deceive unsuspecting souls! Religion is big business these days; where demonically inspired "crooks" use their "charisma" to enhance their bank account and lust for power!

The Third Person of the Trinity is called primarily "the **Holy** Spirit," infiltrating the saint (*hagios* – "holy one") with His character and/or fruit. When God said, "Be ye holy, for I am holy," He was not exhorting us to be God per se, but to be *like* Him ("godly or godlike"); i.e. to reflect God's attribute of holiness; to be separated *to* Christ *from* sin and the world. (cf. Rom. 6) It is in this regard that Paul stresses the "fruit of the Spirit" as "love, joy, peace, longsuffering, gentleness, goodness, faith meekness, temperance [self-control]; against such there is no law." (Gal. 5:22&23) This 9-fold "fruit" reflects the very

Spirit-filled character of Jesus Christ as He walked the earth; now by that same Holy Spirit, the believer can "be like Jesus," walking in Christ's supernatural power; and he adds, "there is no law against" bearing this godly fruit! Religious flesh can never duplicate or counterfeit this Holy Spirit "production" reserved for the true believer.

Love Fulfills the Law

Because of the finished Cross-work of Jesus Christ, we are no longer under the "Old" Covenant (Law), but under the "New" (Grace). Unlike Aaron the high priest, a "new and living way" has been opened, whereby we can enter into the very presence of God; not once a year, or once a month; or even once a day; but in Christ we *live continually* in the Throne Room! (cf. Heb. 10:19&20; Eph. 1:3; 15-20; 3:4-7) In fact, out of that relationship emanates the Spirit's "love" which Scripture declares is *the fulfilling of the law.* Hold everything! How can that be? In Rom. 13, in the context of Civil and social behavior, Paul exhorts us in vs. 9 to "owe no man anything, but to *love one another*; for he that loveth another *hath fulfilled the law.*" (Italics mine) Is Paul actually referring here to the Ten Commandments, etc.? Evidently he is, judging from what follows:

> For this, Thou shalt not commit adultery, Thou shalt not kill, Thou shalt not steal, Thou shalt not bear false witness, Thou shalt not covet; and if there be any other commandment, it is briefly comprehended in this saying, namely, Thou shalt love thy neighbour as thyself. Love worketh no ill to his neighbour; *therefore love is the fulfilling of the law.* (vs. 9, 10; italics mine)

Pentecost places the believer on the "right side" of the Cross through the miraculous "invasion" of the Holy Spirit. What was primarily external obedience to the Law in the Gospels now

106

becomes an internal (inward) reality of a "new" law. This event enables one to bear the Spirit's fruit of love which only desires God's best for his neighbor. If I love that person, I don't want to steal from him or in any way hurt him or his family. If I'm full of God's love, I may not be conscious of the "commandments" as such; rather, there will be an evident and genuine concern for others, produced by the inner-flow of the Holy Spirit. In a godly marriage, for instance, a loving wife need not follow a set of "demands" presented by the husband. If they are both filled with God's love, then the most intimate "demands" will be fulfilled, apart from a list of rules. It presupposes God's redeeming grace operating in our daily lives. Hear Titus 2:11-13:

> For the grace of God that bringeth salvation hath appeared to all men, Teaching us that, denying ungodliness and worldly lusts, we should live soberly, righteously, and godly, in the present world; looking for that Blessed hope, and glorious appearing of the great God and our Saviour Jesus Christ.

CHAPTER 15

GRACE IS NOT LAWLESSNESS

In light of justifying grace (expounded in Rom. 3-5), Paul declares unequivocally; "there is therefore **now** no condemnation to them which are in Christ Jesus..." (Rom. 8:1; emphasis mine) How can that be? I can understand hoping for "no condemnation" someday if I do the right things, but how can I be sure **now**? It must be "hinged" to my relationship to Jesus Christ and what He's already done in my behalf. He alone has removed my "condemnation" freeing me to serve Him; i.e. Jesus Christ became my "Sin Substitute," bearing the full brunt of the Hell that I deserved! He (Jesus) took my place! Hallelujah! This awesome fact must never be treated lightly.

Some scholars hold that Romans 6&7 "unpack" or explain Rom. 5; it's like a commentary where Paul describes our identity and/or position in Christ, along with the struggles of the flesh ("body of sin" Rom. 6;6). In Justification we are saved from the *"penalty* of sin;" while in Sanctification we are being saved from the *"power* of sin." It's clear that both of these truths link directly with Rom. 8:1, declaring our freedom from "condemnation." To have our future security settled in Christ for eternity has great bearing on our ability to overcome sin's power in the present. (cf. John 10:27 & 28; Rom. 6:11-14; 8: 35-39; 1 John 3:1-3)

Furthermore, being "justified by faith" by Christ's Cross-work means the believer is "declared righteous" in God's sight; i.e. when the Father looks at the saint, He sees the righteousness of His Son Jesus Christ! If we can believe this, it's as though the believer *has never sinned*! This is not to say that believers (saints) do not sin, but because of God's imputed righteousness the sinner stands perfect before the Lord.

Christ My Righteousness

"Imputation" is a bookkeeping term, meaning to transfer or credit a payment to someone's account. In this case, Christ has paid the price of the sinner's redemption (deliverance) which is personally received or applied by faith. For instance, if I owe a huge bank debt and they call for the payment immediately, what am I to do if I'm broke? Suppose, in the face of impending bankruptcy, a dear friend hears of my dilemma and offers to wire the money to the bank in my behalf. I can't pay back my friend *or* the bank! What do I do? I humbly accept my friend's offer to pay what I could not pay. The bank accepts the check and credits my account, declaring the debt "paid in full." My account is "settled" forever, even though I didn't pay it personally, for my Friend paid it in my behalf. Wow! That's what Jesus did with my "sin debt" and now I'm "justified;" i.e. declared righteous in God's sight. (Justified—just-as-if-I-died to pay the full penalty of my sin) In other words, my *sins* were "imputed" to Christ on the Cross, so that by faith His *righteousness* could be "imputed" to me! Praise God! So unbelievable, yet so true!

A New Law Introduced

Some would ignorantly infer that being saved by grace (Eph. 2:8) or being justified by faith without works promotes "easy-believism" or a license to sin; we must clarify that to be free from the Law of Moses does not make one "lawless." Even the glorious reality of "no condemnation" in Christ (Rom. 8:1) grants no excuse for sinning. Such a transforming liberation does not in any way grant license to do wrong, but rather a freedom and empowerment to do right! Now the "empowerment" comes through a "new law" described in Rom. 8:2, "for the *law of the Spirit of life* in Christ Jesus hath made me free from the *law of sin and death.*" (Italics mine)

110

There are actually two "laws" mentioned here. In our unregenerate (unsaved) state we were under "the law of sin and death;" being then birthed into Christ, we are placed under "the law of the Spirit of life;" i.e. we now have "**life** over **death**," and "**the Spirit** over **sin**!" Christ put "death to death," removing our condemnation and granting eternal life. In the second law, He has provided the power of sanctification (godliness) by means of the indwelling Holy Spirit's victory over sin. Think of it, because of the Cross, the Resurrection, the Ascension, and Pentecost, we have **life** over **death** and **the Spirit** over **sin**! Amen!

Wright Brother's Discovery

While teaching in Atlanta for several years, I often drove after class to the Hartville Airport to "chill out" by watching huge jets land. I parked right on the edge of the field where I "experienced" the incessant roar and smell of giant aircraft. They flew constantly over my head, never failing to "rattle" the car and my body. I thought so often of the Wright Brothers who got this thing started, at the price of failures, frustration and ridicule. They finally launched the "Kitty Hawk" in 1903 and the rest is history.

Did Orville and Wilbur invent a new law that could sustain man in flight, or did they "discover" an already existing law? It's clear that the law of Aerodynamics was operating all along (e.g. birds, etc.), making it possible to temporarily "defy" the law of gravity. So it is that God "introduced" a "new law" in Christ's redemptive work, discovered by the Apostle Paul by divine revelation! Pentecost was the means of dispensing "the Spirit of Life" in Christ Jesus to every genuine believer. Thus, we are no longer "grounded" under the load of sin; but through the Spirit of Christ, we can "soar in the Heavenlies" (cf. Eph. 1:15-20). Yes, the Holy Spirit has granted us grace to "defy" or overcome sin's power here and now; however, the true believer who has "fought the good fight" longs for that Glorious Day when sin will be totally removed forever. Amen!

To put it another way, when Christ died, we died with Him; when He was buried, we were buried with Him; when He rose from the grave, we arose with Him; and when He ascended to Heaven, we ascended with Him to "sit together in heavenly places." (cf. Rom. 6; Gal. 2:20; Eph. 2:6) Being "born again" is to be birthed from "above" (cf. John3:3 with 3:31), making us "heavenly citizens" joined to Christ by the Spirit. This is God's Truth, whether I appropriate it by faith or not. The "Gospel plane" is available for "takeoff," and I need to get "onboard" by faith and enjoy the ride! We have everything we need to live this Christian life by virtue of the reality of Pentecost!

The Law Fulfilled In Us

Having established our position of grace under the "new law" of the "Spirit of life" (Rom. 8:2), let's take it a step further. The Scripture goes on to say, "For what the law could not do...God sending his own Son in the likeness of sinful flesh, and for sin, condemned sin in the flesh" (Rom. 8:3); i.e. Jesus not only took the condemning penalty of the law in His death, but fulfilled all of the law in *His life*. Why? "[So] that the righteousness of the law might be fulfilled *in* us... (8:4; emphasis mine).

Returning to Romans 8:2-4, Paul explains the inability of the law to save from sin; therefore, Jesus "condemned sin the flesh;" i.e. in life He conquered sin (being sinless), and in death He forever paid the full penalty of man's sin; thus, the result is described in vs. 4; i.e. "that the righteousness of the law might be fulfilled in us..." Notice, it doesn't say that the righteousness of the law is fulfilled *by* us, but *in* us. How can that be? Because of Pentecost, the One who fulfilled the law totally now lives within us and we are *complete in Him* (Col. 2:10).The perfect standing and fulfillment of the law is afforded the believer by virtue of being in Christ. In addition, the condemning

112

"handwriting of ordinances" (i.e. the Moral Law) was "blotted out" (removed), being "nailed to His Cross!" (Col. 2:13&14) He totally eradicated my "rap sheet!" forever! (Rom. 8:1) This glorious work of grace now enables the believer to live on the **right side** of the Cross.

"Better" Covenant

No wonder Hebrews extols the New Testament sacrificial "once-for-all" work of Christ as "better." The Mosaic Law was essential under the Old Covenant; but Christ's perfect sacrifice fulfilled the Old and ushered in the "dispensation of grace." (Eph. 3:2) The old system was "good" (adequate at the time); but the "new" covenant was "better." Both covenants were ordained by the same God, who revealed Himself progressively. We have a fuller revelation than Old Testament believers; and thus we have a "greater" personal intimacy, understanding, privilege and responsibility.

This definitely has bearing on the "greater works" mentioned by Jesus, whose ministry was basically confined to Israel's borders; it's said that He probably never travelled more than 100 miles from "home." Now there would be a potential "army" of Spirit-controlled witnesses reaching across the world after Pentecost. What began with the Son of God would now be multiplied by many sons of God under the auspices (dispensing) of the Holy Spirit!

CHAPTER 16
PRAYER AND PENTECOST

A true believer prays much more than he realizes. One of the evidences of the inward ministry of the Spirit's intercessory work is enabling us to pray "according to the will of God." (Rom. 8:27) Due to this new law of "the Spirit of life in Christ Jesus (Rom. 8:2)," the believer now has the Paraclete (lit. "One called alongside"); i.e. the Spirit Himself, mediating before the Father with "groanings which cannot be uttered" or expressed verbally. In the context of present suffering and the future hope of Christ's Coming, he (Paul) describes how this divine "transaction" works in behalf of the yielded saint:

> *Likewise the Spirit also helpeth our infirmities; for we know not what we should pray for as we ought; but the Spirit itself maketh intercession for us with groanings which cannot be uttered. And he that searcheth the hearts knoweth what is the mind of the Spirit, because he maketh intercession for the saints according to the will of God.* (Rom. 8:26, 27) (italics mine)

Could it be said that true prayer doesn't originate with the believer for "we know not what we should pray for..." It is the Holy Spirit who "prompts" (prods) our hearts "according to the will of God;" i.e. prayer originates with God and is communicated to the saint by the Spirit. The believer in turn prays to the Father in Jesus Name. This concept was expounded by Jesus in John 16:12ff but the disciples were not yet prepared to receive it. He said:

> I have yet many things to say unto you, but ye cannot hear [understand] them now...Howbeit when he, the Spirit of truth is come [i.e.

115

Pentecost], he will guide you into all truth… (vs. 12, 13)

In vs. 23, Jesus says, (referring to Pentecost) "In that day ye shall ask me nothing…Whatsoever ye shall ask the Father in my name, he will give it you." So now with the illumination and intercession of the Holy Spirit the believer can address the Father, praying in Jesus' Name! It seems to me that this takes the so-called "Lord's Prayer" to a different level; i.e. unctionized now by the indwelling Holy Spirit. To summarize: Genuine prayer is "instigated" by the Holy Spirit in the believer who then prays to the Father in Jesus' Name!

It must be emphasized that this process is not automatic or unrelated to the believer's spiritual condition. One cannot "pray in the Spirit" without walking in the Spirit. "…The effectual fervent prayer of a righteous man availeth much." (Jas.5:16) We can't pray any higher than we live; which is to say that obedience and faith are essential to effective prayer. (cf. Prov. 3:5&6)

Evidently, prayer is more than "saying" or memorizing a written prayer. Most religions have some form of prayer or means of addressing their deities (gods). That God-consciousness is instilled in every person (Gen. 2:7), but is darkened and perverted by sin; this accounts for the myriad of religious expressions of "prayer" from man's fallen nature. That changes when the Holy Spirit regenerates a sinner and his spirit (heart) is "made alive" and divinely "connected" to the true and living God! Prayer is now a result of a living, genuine relationship with Christ.

Is it possible that even the Church has relegated prayer to some "religious exercise" or format? Is prayer to be something "tacked on" to our lives or part of a daily routine regulated by the clock? Personally, I have wrestled through the years with this matter of true prayer. How often I cried with the disciples, "Lord, teach me to pray!" I've read of the spiritual "giants" in

Church history who spent hours on end in prayer, and envied their spiritual "stamina;" after all, prayer was the basis of their effectiveness and spiritual success, and I've longed for that.

I heard that Martin Luther, of Reformation fame (1535), said he had so much work to do that he could not make it on less than "three hours of prayer daily." Today we might say, "Are you kidding?" But I took things like that seriously, suffering enormous frustration and defeat trying to be a Martin Luther or someone else. I've concluded that I can't "borrow" another believer's prayer life. I have my own unique identity in Christ, who deals with me accordingly. My ultimate incentive must be to obey God, walking in constant fellowship with Him. Again, we cannot pray any higher than we live. To "walk in the Spirit" is to "pray in the Spirit!"

Use of Scriptural Prayers

Please understand that I'm in no way being critical of these noble servants of yesteryear whose prayers were mightily used to extend God's Kingdom. They were unique men of God for their time, unctionized with God's burden. To try to "copy" their style, intensity, or time-frame, etc. would be an exercise in futility. By all means meditate on the prayers of King David, Nehemiah, Daniel, Ezra, the Reformers, the Puritans, etc., but you can't really "pray" their prayers per se. They were not performing some "religious" exercise, but were expressing the God-given burden that was bursting in *their* hearts. So evidently genuine, effective prayer emanates (stems) out of a heart in intimate communion with God by the Holy Spirit; thus, praying according to the will of God. No mere outward religious format here!

As previously mentioned, I've considered the so-called "Lord's Prayer" in this light. Jesus came as the Messiah to establish His Kingdom on earth; thus He taught them to pray a "kingdom" prayer; e.g. "...Thy will be done on earth as it is in Heaven..." I

117

would never criticize the believer's use of this legitimate prayer, but this was "pre-Pentecost;" i.e. the indwelling intercessory ministry of the Holy Spirit had not yet occurred. Significantly, while Jesus speaks often of the "kingdom" in the Gospels, he never mentions the "Body of Christ"(Church) per se; that is totally a Pauline revelation or "mystery." (cf. Rom. 16:25; Eph. 3:9; 5:32; Col. 1:26, 27) My point is that the indwelling Power of Pentecost places the N.T. saint on another level of personal intimacy in prayer. A "new and living way is opened" into God's presence through Christ's atonement; now it's possible to "pray without ceasing" (1 Thess. 5:17) rather than just repeating prayers in a "closet." There's no conflict here, for both of these "modes" of prayer are still valid and compensatory.

How often I've attended a prayer meeting where a list of "prayer requests" were offered, but never mentioned in prayer. Did folks just "forget" the request, or was the witness of the Spirit missing? In reality, it's difficult to enter into another's request or burden without the Spirit's preparation. It's like trying to sing someone else's "song;" you can possibly relate, but it doesn't really match your personal experience. So effective prayer does not originate through a mere earthly request, but really originates in Heaven. By His Spirit (Rom. 8:26), God intercedes in prompting and enabling our hearts to pray according to His will. John makes it clear that if we pray according to His (God's) will, He *hears and answers us.* (1John. 5:14) Again, I'm not suggesting that we stop praying for one another's requests; certainly God can instantly burden our hearts for that individual's need, etc. We're speaking here of God's "ideal" plan in the midst of our human imperfection.

Consider also, that since prayer originates with God; could it be that we are praying in our spirit while being totally unaware of it? Otherwise, how can we obey Jesus' command that, "men ought *always* to pray, and not to faint." (Lk. 18:1) What about Paul's afore-mentioned exhortation to "pray without ceasing?"

If prayer is just a conscious recitation to God or time spent in the "closet," when would we get any work done, etc.? It seems to me that prayer is the result of an intimate, saving relationship with God; the life-line communication of the saint with his Savior, motivated and sustained by Holy-Ghost intervention. (c.f. Phil. 4:6-7) Notice how this is typified by the tabernacle's altar of "perpetual (non-ending) incense" (Ex. 30:8).

Must we always be conscious of this divine activity? Rarely are we aware of our heart beat, yet that doesn't stop it from functioning. Likewise, it's been said that "prayer is to the soul, what breath is to the body." If we had to consciously "crank" our lung activity, we'd be dead in no time! Can I suggest that prayer is not only an *activity*, but an *attitude*? May I reiterate that true prayer originates from the Father to the believer by the Holy Spirit who reveals God's will; the saint now "prays in the Spirit," in the authority of Jesus' Name, and the cycle of the Spirit's intercession is completed before the Father. Amen.

Intercession Illustrated

A powerful example and type of prayer intercession is found in Exodus 17:8ff where Israel was confronted in battle by the Amalekites. Moses commands Joshua to choose an army of men to fight Amalek, while he (Moses) stands "on top of the hill" with God's "rod" of authority in his hand. As the battle ensues, Moses stands with his hands "held up" in intercession for victory; this causes Israel to "prevail;" but when he got tired and let down his hands, Amalek prevailed. He needed help!

Significantly, two priests accompanied Moses to the mount to minister to him in this time of distress. Aaron and Hur took a stone and placed it under the weary Moses so he could sit. In turn, they each took one of Moses' hands, lifting it high toward Heaven. It says that these hands were held "steady until the going down of the sun!" Through this intercession of the intercessor (Moses), the battle was won. Joshua fought just as valiantly whether Moses' hands were "up or down;" but Israel only prevailed when his hands were raised in effective intercession. How this illustrates the difference that true intercession (prayer) makes! How can we apply this today in the Body of Christ?

We've already looked at the Holy Spirit's ministry of intercession in Rom. 8:26 where He *"helpeth* our infirmities..." We no longer have an "Aaron and Hur" team standing with us, as did Moses; rather we have God the Spirit Himself living within us who is constantly "helping" us in prayer. And this is also in the context of spiritual warfare in the heavenlies as opposed to Moses' earthly conflict.

The Greek word used here for "help" is remarkable; it is transliterated: *sunantilambanomai,* a participle, literally meaning to "continually hold up the other end of the load with us." Yes, that's the idea of the non-ending Spirit's ministry of "helping our infirmities." We have a built-in divine "Aaron and Hur" priestly intercession! How good it that? Mr. Spurgeon adds, "You have a glorious *helper*—the Holy Ghost---and by His power you may accomplish miracles of holiness." This provision of spiritual enablement is yet another glorious benefit resulting from Pentecost.

CHAPTER 17

PRAYER AND SPIRITUAL WARFARE

Significantly, this intercessory work of the Spirit is intricately connected to the believer's armor in fighting the forces of Hell. (cf. Eph. 6:10-19) After depicting all the "parts" of the armor (e.g. breastplate, shield, helmet, etc.), Paul adds:

> Praying always with all prayer and supplication in the Spirit, and watching thereunto with all perseverance and supplication for all saints; And for me, that utterance may be given unto me, that I may open my mouth boldly, to make known the mystery of the gospel (Eph. 6:18, 19).

Well, what's prayer have to do with victory in the battle? Everything! Evidently prayer is the capstone of the armor or the "grease" that lubricates the weapons of warfare! Matthew Henry says that "prayer must buckle on all the other parts of our Christian armour." "Praying always [lit. in all seasons or every occasion] with all [kinds of] prayer and supplication [supply] in the Spirit..." Prayer is more than just "asking and receiving "or "a little talk with Jesus;" it is the believer's ongoing, intimate, communication pipeline with the Lord Himself! It is the means by which the "whole armour" is appropriated and utilized against the incessant attacks of Satan's fiery darts (missiles). Right here is the heart of whether the saint lives in victory or defeat!

The Sword of the Spirit

We could camp here for a long time, but let me briefly comment on "the Sword of the Spirit, which is the word of God." (vs.17) The "helmet of salvation" deals primarily with our acknowledged position or identity in Christ. Satan's ongoing enterprise through demons, etc. is to "accuse us day and night" or to "talk us out of" our salvation (security) in Christ. That's where the "shield of faith" (vs. 16) must be utilized to dispel the barrage of doubts, fears, etc. How? By the prayerful and confident use of the "Sword of the Spirit," the Word!

It's essential to note that the "word of God" here is not the usual Greek word *logos*, expressing the full revelation of Scripture; but here it is the word *rhema*, which is a specific word (message) from the "Word" (logos) for a specific situation and/or person. For instance, Jesus countered Satan's attack in the wilderness with Scripture fit for the occasion. He didn't just say, "I'm the Word," or "read the Bible." Likewise, the believer prayerfully resists the enemy "by faith," being confident of who he is in Christ); (cf. 1 Pet. 5: 8&9; Jas. 4:7); he then uses the Sword or Word (rhema) to "cut off" the "serpent's" head! This strategy places great demand for the believer to be both filled with the Spirit (discernment) and a working knowledge of the Bible. Pentecost makes this possible.

John reveals Satan as a "deceiver" (liar) and "the accuser of our brethren;" (cf. Rev. 12:9&10) Satan hates the Truth (Christ) and the Body of Christ (Truth-bearers); his ploy is to slander the eternal God and the marvelous Salvation which He (God) has imbedded in every believer's heart. Ephesians is replete with references of the saint's heavenly position "in Christ." The Enemy desires to "pull us out of the sky," replacing faith with doubt and fear; this leads to discouragement and defeat which further hinders the spirit of prayer. Unbelief slanders the character of God who has made full provision for the saint's victory.

The Devil is the "father of lies" (John 8:44) and he has duped the majority of Christendom. I maintain that our so-called "Bible believing" churches are filled with saints, including the leadership, who live defeated, ineffective lives, while "praying for national revival." That's an exercise in futility. Evangelism wanes in such an atmosphere, for without personal "revival" our "light" is dim at best and we cease to be "appetizers" for Jesus. We are called to be "fishers of men" which necessitates bait that attracts; it could be said that we are that "worm" on the end of the hook "wiggling" for Jesus; and be assured that no fish likes a dead worm!

Effective Prayer for Others

Paul's reference here to the "weapon of prayer" is not simply for personal victory but a means of intercession for others; i.e. "all saints." (6:18) There is "one Body" (the Church--Eph.4:4) which means we're all in this battle together. We are intricately joined just as parts of the physical body and need each other to properly function. (cf. 1 Cor.12) The chain is only as strong as its weakest link. A football team is "linked" together as one. When one player fails it affects the whole team. We *are* our "brother's keeper;" thus we prayerfully stand in the gap in behalf of fellow saints who are struggling to serve God in the midst of a Satan-infested world. (cf. 1 Tim. 2:1; Jas. 5:16)

But notice that this is a "warfare" prayer; i.e. "watching…with all perseverance and supplication…" This entails being "alert" and awake (discerning) of other's needs and how the Enemy is attacking. This is much more involved than, "Lord, bless the missionaries" kind of thing. The tough part is the "persevering" and relentless (never give up) attitude to stand firm in behalf of the brethren. Wow, what a seeming impossible assignment! One thing is certain, such a task is impossible apart from a personal, Spirit-filled relationship with Christ. Again, that is possible because of Pentecost!

Finally, and significantly, Paul includes himself personally in requesting the saint's prayers; "and [pray] for me," he says, "that utterance may be given unto me, that I may open my mouth boldly, to make known the mystery of the Gospel." (Eph. 6:19) Yes, Paul obviously experienced first-hand the Enemy's effort to "shut his mouth" from proclaiming the Gospel. The average saint is not the only one under demonic attack. He (Satan) desires to "take down" every true preacher, robbing him of the ability to preach the Word eloquently and boldly! This is so apropos for churches today where sermons are often merely academic, irrelevant, boring, and powerless! Paul knew that preaching was futile without the unction of the Holy Spirit.

The pastor must be both a teacher and a preacher. As a teacher he expounds and opens (unpacks) the Scriptures with application, etc. As a preacher, however, he takes that same Scripture and boldly "storms the listener's will" in order to motivate an immediate response and personal commitment to the message. Someone was asked if the great 18th Century evangelist George Whitefield ever gave "invitations" at the end of his sermons; he said, "no, but his *whole sermon* was an invitation!" He preached during a time of "great awakening" when preachers were "on fire" for God and people gathered to "watch them burn!" Lord, do it again!

There may be a place for "sharing", as we say, but not in the pulpit. Paul ends his earthly journey by exhorting Timothy to: "preach the Word; be instant [ready] in season and out of season; reprove, rebuke, exhort with all longsuffering and doctrine." (2 Tim. 4:2) Now that's preaching, my friend! But this kind of preaching is only found in churches that understand and practice mutual intercession of "all prayer" for "all saints," and especially the pastor/preacher. This would curb much of the present-day compromise, worldliness, and emaciated excuses for ministry; moreover, it would greatly diminish the epidemic of pastoral scandals and "drop outs" (defections) that plague the church today. Yes, we need an awakening in America, but for starters we need true "revival" and reformation in the Church; i.e. a restoration of godly repentance (turning to God from sin) accompanied by a restoration of Biblical Doctrine and godly living. Again, this is all made possible because of Pentecost **now**.

CHAPTER 18

RECEIVING GOD'S FULLNESS

We need to conclude our study by considering how to rightly utilize the "power of Pentecost" in light of present day confusion. A man said to me one time, "I'm a Christian, but I'm seekin' the Holy Ghost." Did he mean that he had God the Father and God the Son, but not God the Spirit? If so, then he could not be a Christian according to Rom. 8:9, which says "...if any man have not the Spirit of Christ, he is none of his;" i.e. anyone who doesn't possess the Spirit does not belong to God. Plus the fact, it is the Holy Spirit Himself who regenerates or "births" the believer into the Body of Christ. (cf. John 3:8; Tit. 3:5) Probably the man meant that he was seeking the "baptism of the Spirit;" but, as we've stressed, the believer has already been "baptized" by the Spirit into the Body. (cf. 1 Cor. 12:13) Then how about "being filled with the Spirit?" That certainly makes more Biblical sense, but still needs to be clarified.

Sold-Out Attitude

Paul says, "Be not drunk with wine...but be filled [lit. *be being full*] with the Spirit." (Eph.5:18; italics mine). As we've already discussed, "be filled" is not an action so much as a condition; i.e. a state of being fully controlled by the Spirit. We must remember that the Holy Spirit is a Person who desires to lead and empower every aspect of our lives. The issue is not "getting more" of the Spirit, for we have All of Him via Pentecost; rather the question is does He have all of us? It makes a difference how a Christian lives. Sin (disobedience) "grieves" the Holy Spirit, "quenching" His full blessing. (cf. Eph. 4:30; 1 Thess. 5:19)

I think the prerequisite of "walking in the fullness of the Spirit" is connected to Paul's exhortation in Rom. 12:1&2; he pleads "by the mercies of God;" i.e. all of His provisions previously expounded; "that ye present your bodies a living sacrifice, holy, acceptable unto God;" i.e. dead to self and alive (separated) unto God. That entails not being "conformed [adapted to, sucked into] this world" (and its satanic philosophy); "but [alla - on the contrary] be ye transformed [i.e. changing, growing] by the renewing of your mind [spirit, heart]..."

D. L. Moody believed that "the moment our hearts are emptied of selfishness and ambition and self-seeking and everything that is contrary to God's Law [Word], the Holy Spirit will come and fill every corner of our hearts."

Adelaide Pollard captured this theme in the following hymn:

> Have Thine own way, Lord! Have Thine own way! Thou art the Potter; I am the clay. Mould me and make me after Thy will, While I am waiting, Yielded and still.
> Have Thine own way, Lord! Have Thine own way! Hold o'er my being absolute sway! Fill with Thy Spirit 'Till all shall see Christ only, always, Living in me!"

It then behooves us to "let the Word of Christ dwell in you [us] richly with all wisdom... (Col. 3:16); or as David declared, "Thy Word have I hid [treasured up] in mine heart that I might not sin against Thee." (Psa.119:11) He (David) also extols the person who is "blessed" (happy) by "not walking in the counsel [advice] of the ungodly..." but rather "delights" in the Word, "meditating" in it "day and night." (Psa. 1:1&2) To be saturated with the Word of God is to begin thinking like God thinks!

Servant of Christ, the power of God is resident in the Word of God. What you do with the Word is what God will do with you! Paul told us to "preach the Word," not just *about* the Word. He said that in 2 Tim. 4:2 in the context of his horrific description of the "last days" (2 Tim. 3). As we anticipate the Lord's Return, it's imperative that we faithfully expound the whole Counsel of God (the Bible) in the power of the Holy Spirit!

We need to be reminded in these days how unique, incomparable, and indispensable is the Bible-- The Word of God. Someone has beautifully and succinctly described God's Word thusly:

> This book contains the mind of God, the state of man, the way of Salvation, the doom of sinners, and the happiness of believers. Its doctrines are holy, its precepts are binding, its histories are true, and its decisions are immutable.
> Read it to be wise, believe it to be safe, and practice it to be holy. It contains light to direct you, food to support you, and comfort to cheer you. It is the traveler's map, the pilgrim's staff, the pilot's compass, the soldier's sword, and the Christian's charter.
> Here paradise is restored, Heaven opened, and the gates of Hell disclosed. Christ is its grand Object; our good is its design, and the glory of God its end.
> It should fill the memory, rule the heart, and guide the feet. Read it slowly, frequently, and prayerfully. It is given you in life, and will be opened in the judgment, and be remembered forever. It involves the highest responsibility, will reward the greatest labor, and condemn all who trifle with its sacred contents.

> Unknown

Taking the Spirit's Power by Faith

In closing, I want to be careful to not suggest that there's some "mystic formula" for being "filled" with the Spirit; I submit, however, that Scripture bids the believer come in simple faith as a child receiving his father's gift or provision. I think of a dad who holds out a gift to his child, freely offering it by saying "take it, take it" while the child continues to "plead" for it. Sadly, many sincere saints continue to plead for what the Father has already given! For many years I had my own little "ritual" before preaching the Word. I would kneel at my pulpit chair, squeeze my eyes and begin "begging" God to anoint me with the Spirit. I was sincere, as are many who do similar things; and, knowing my heart, God blessed me in spite of my ignorance. Eventually He showed me a "better" way; i.e. just reaching out to the Lord in simple faith, and receiving the power of Pentecost which He has already given me.

I think it's significant that babies are typically born "fully equipped;" i.e. they have all the body parts they need up front. For instance, I've watched an infant staring at his raised hand, as if to say, "What's that?" It's only a matter time before he discovers what that hand can do (good or bad). The point is, that he "possesses" the hand before he utilizes it; he begins to appropriate or use something that he's had from the start. So it is that as believers we appropriate by faith the Holy Spirit's power which we've possessed from the "new birth" or regeneration. What then is the "filling" or so-called "second (or third) blessing," but a definite act of faith, appropriating the power of Pentecost to fulfill a God-given task.

During one of those times of struggle to "get the Spirit's power," I heard a great preacher from Ireland pray this unforgettable prayer just prior to his message: He boldly lifted his voice and exclaimed, **"I take the Promised Holy Ghost; the Blessed Power of Pentecost to fill me to the uttermost; I**

take, thank God, He undertakes!" That prayer (declaration) pierced my heart! I began to utilize it in preparing my heart to preach. What renewal and liberation came to my soul and ministry! Thank God for the awesome privilege of being a recipient of this magnificent provision of Pentecost to meet the challenge of these "last days."

CONCLUSION

A modern-day prophet, A. W. Tozer (1897-1963) stated that "The Spirit-filled life is not a special, deluxe edition of Christianity. It is part and parcel of the total plan of God for His people." That being said, it's a shame to witness the inferior, emaciated spiritual condition of the present-day Church. We have been "invaded" by compromise and carnality whereby the "Spirit-filled" believer is a rarity. The Church is so "subnormal" spiritually that a "normal" Spirit-filled Christian is considered "abnormal!" God help us!

Plea for Biblical Harmony

We have been satanically side-tracked by worldly pursuits, politics, racial divide, social media, etc. which have hindered our united witness as "ambassadors for Christ."(cf. 2 Cor. 5:19&20) All the "fuss" about "racial reconciliation," etc. needs to be taken to the Cross, where the "middle wall of partition" was eternally broken down! Paul states this truth clearly in Ephesians 2:13-16:

> But now in Christ Jesus ye who sometimes were far off are made nigh by the blood of Christ. For he is our peace, who hath made both one, and hath broken down the middle wall of partition between us; Having abolished in his flesh the enmity, even the law of commandments contained in ordinances; for to make in himself of twain one new man, so making peace; And that he might reconcile both unto God in one body by the cross, having slain the enmity thereby.

Not only Jews and gentiles but all believers (regardless of ethnicity) are made one in the Body of Christ. Jesus died for only one "race", the Adamic (human) race; "for as in Adam all

131

die, even so in Christ shall all be made alive." (1 Cor. 15:22) Paul further exhorts us that the practice of this "unity" is not automatic; but one that takes humility with "longsuffering, forbearing one another in love; *endeavoring to keep the unity* of the Spirit in the bond of peace,[for] *there is one body* and one Spirit..." (cf. Eph. 4:2-4; italics mine) Like any other relationship in our lives, we need to "work at it" (e.g. marriage, family, ministry, etc.); but, thankfully, we're not called to "make (produce) unity" in the Body, because that's already been done by the Holy Spirit. Ours is to "endeavor [lit. be careful, diligent] to keep [preserve] the unity..." (cf. Eph. 4:3) and that requires walking in the Spirit.

Over the years I have preached side by side with godly ministers of color who firmly believed that the basic issue with mankind is "not skin, but *sin*." Our communities will not be changed without the Spirit's conviction and conversion of the individuals in that community. So let's get on with the main business at hand; i.e. proclaiming the glorious Gospel of the Lord Jesus Christ to a lost world in the power of the Holy Spirit!

Consequently, this thesis stresses that it's Pentecost **now**! The Holy Spirit's work continues right on schedule according to God's plan. We don't need to "go back", nor can we! Even during the 400 "silent years" between the Old and New Covenants, the Spirit was operating. His plan has never been altered. We must learn to live in the present, not the past or future. That's the key to victory. The Lord is the Great I AM, emphasizing the "present" tense. Focusing on the *past* can lead to depression; while obsession with the *future* fosters anxiety and ungodly fear (oppression). Pentecost secured ongoing, personal "revival" to the believer despite what may be going on in the world.

I'm not sure that Paul conducted "revival meetings" per se; but rather he "preached the Word...in season and out of season," being assured that God's message would succeed in every circumstance. He confidently praises God who "always casueth us to triumph in Christ...a sweet savour of Christ, in them that are saved, and in them that perish." (2 Cor. 2:14f) We learn here that as we preach the Word, God's purpose is being fulfilled in both the saved and the lost! This is the case whether there's a so-called "awakening" or a "move of God" or not. In a recent film on George Mueller, a quote by William Booth of Salvation Army fame caught my eye: He said, "I'm not waiting for a move of God, *I am a move of God*!" It's "Pentecost Now;" thus, we can "brighten the corner where we are," despite our situation or perception. The Spirit is Sovereign, and He has stated that His spoken Word "shall not return unto me void, but it shall accomplish that which I please, and it shall prosper in the thing whereto I sent it." (Isa. 55:11) Amen!

Can America be "Revived"?

In light of our present-day political corruption and religious apostasy, can God once again bring another "great awakening" to our land? Absolutely! Should we pray to that end? Absolutely! In fact, if we're living in the reality of Pentecost, our united prayers for a "spiritual outpouring" should be effective. (e.g. James 5:16) The nature and scope of that "move of God," of course, would certainly be His prerogative. I wouldn't think, however, that such a "move" would not simply "multiply" the existing, watered-down, compromised version of so-called evangelicalism; rather, we need a "reformation" of true Biblical doctrine preached with the "Holy Ghost (fire) sent down from heaven..." (1 Pet.1:12); likewise, we need an "epidemic" of "refired" (revived) saints whose lives genuinely reflect the character of Jesus Christ in this hostile world! (cf. 2 Cor. 5:17-21)

While many feel that since prophetically we're facing the soon-return of Christ, widespread "revival" is out of the picture. I understand that mentality, and yet only God knows the specific time-frame; certainly, we're to "occupy [work] until He comes." We don't know just how much time we have left in the harvest field, but the time frame and results are "in His hands." A mighty ingathering (harvest) of souls may be on the horizon, just prior to His Coming. In fact, despite the encroaching Satanic forces of Communism and paganism etc., there are reports of a significant ingathering of souls being saved across the world. Thankfully, the Word of God is not bound!

I also anticipate the reviving of "pockets of grace" scattered throughout our country; I'm referring to remnant groups (churches) of true believers, shining brightly for Jesus and thus prepared for the "Catching up of the Bride of Christ" into Glory. (cf. 1 Thess. 4:13ff) Yes, another Holy Spirit "revival" might be God's means in fully preparing His church for that great event. After all, as an old mentor used to quip, "Jesus, the Bridegroom, is not coming back for a bald, buck-toothed, bow-legged Bride; but one 'prepared as a bride adorned for her husband.'" (cf. Rev. 21:2) Even so come, Lord Jesus!

Ultimately, the reality and purpose of Pentecost was more than the Spirit's indwelling presence, His power, gifts, understanding, etc. Beyond these essentials given to the disciples, Jesus emphasized that the Spirit would "not speak of himself, but whatsoever he shall hear, that shall he speak...*He shall glorify me;* for he shall receive of mine, and shall shew it unto you." (John16: 13-14; italics mine)

Clearly, the Spirit's ministry was to focus solely upon Christ the Son; i.e. to "glorify" (*doxadzo*, to exalt, magnify) Him alone! Just as Jesus glorified the Father (cf. John 17:1-5), so the Spirit was to glorify the Son! The Spirit did not come to glorify Himself, although some would infer otherwise by their preoccupation with His "gifts and power;" in so doing they miss the Star of Pentecost; i.e. Jehovah Jesus! To keep emphasizing "the Spirit" will lead to fanaticism and emotional confusion. Likewise, to constantly emphasize or focus on the Father, will lead to the heresy of Universalism; i.e. all people are God's children or "saved;" however, because of the indwelling Spirit of Christ, we can "talk about Jesus the Son" morning, noon, and night, only to be drawn closer to God! Hallelujah, what a Savior!

A closing thought: How do believers on a practical level "glorify" Christ in this dark world? What does that look like? I heard one teacher "define" it as living our daily lives in such a way that everything we are and do "makes **Him**, Jesus Christ, look **Great!**" (emphasis mine) As "children of light" we are "reflectors" of His image. This kind of light cannot be hidden from the world. That's what "revival" looks like! O, for such an "epidemic" to break out in this day!

A.B. Simpson, previously mentioned as a leader during the Welsh Revival (1904), captured the ultimate theme and purpose of Pentecost in a hymn called "Himself:"

> Once it was the blessing, **now** it is the Lord;
> Once it was the feeling, **now** it is His Word;
> Once His gift I wanted, **now**, the Giver own;
> Once I sought for healing, **now** Himself alone.
>
> Once 'twas painful trying, **now** 'tis perfect trust;
> Once a half salvation, **now** the uttermost;
> Once 'twas ceaseless holding, **now** He holds me fast;
> Once 'twas constant drifting, **now** my anchor's cast.

Once 'twas busy planning, **now** 'tis trustful prayer;
Once 'twas anxious caring, **now** He has the care;
Once 'twas what I wanted, **now** what Jesus says;
Once 'twas constant asking, **now** 'tis ceaseless praise.

Once it was my working, His it hence shall be;
Once I tried to use Him, **now** He uses me;
Once the pow'r I wanted, **now** the Mighty One;
Once for self I labored, **now** for Him alone.
(emphasis mine)

POST SCRIPT: THIS IS THE AMAZING <u>NOW</u> PROVISION OF PENTECOST!

ABOUT THE AUTHOR

Pastor, teacher, author, mentor, and presently a Bible instructor at the Rescue Mission of Mahoning Valley in Youngstown, Ohio. Bill Finnigan has been engaged in active ministry for almost sixty years.

A native of Newark, New Jersey, Bill received a call to ministry while in college. The ensuing years were spent in intensive study to learn and sharpen ministry skills. Attending several universities, he holds a number of degrees, including the Master of Divinity and Doctor of Ministry. For over twenty seven years, Bill has held pulpits in Pennsylvania and New Jersey, reaching people with God's life-changing Word.

His outreach has also included radio, prison, and Bible conference ministries. He has served as a college professor, and director of a Biblical counseling center. He has authored other publications, including Healing for the Mind, which offers comfort and remedy for mental turmoil; Forgiven to Forgive, which serves as an antidote to resentment and bitterness; Living Skillfully, a commentary on the book of Proverbs; and Facing Depression, examining its cause and cure.

More recently his time has been devoted to writing, preaching, and the on-going Biblical instruction at the rescue mission in Youngstown. As the Lord provides opportunities, he continues to be busily engaged in the Lord's Vineyard, considering himself "refired," rather than retired.

Dr. William J. Finnigan
8883 Sherwood Dr. NE
Warren, Ohio 44484
email: bilfinn1@yahoo.com
website: billfinnigan.com